FAMILY
Love

Alfred H. Ells

FAMILY *Love*

WHAT WE NEED,

WHAT WE SEEK,

WHAT WE MUST CREATE

OLIVER
NELSON

THOMAS NELSON PUBLISHERS
Nashville • Atlanta • London • Vancouver

Copyright © 1995 by Alfred H. Ells

Every effort has been made to contact the owners or owners' agents of copyrighted material for permission to use their material. If copyrighted material has been included without the correct copyright notice or without permission, due to error or failure to locate owners/agents or otherwise, we apologize for the error or omission and ask that the owner or owner's agent contact Thomas Nelson and supply appropriate information. Correct information will be included in any reprinting.

Published in Nashville, Tennessee, by Thomas Nelson, Inc., Publishers, and distributed in Canada by Word Communications, Ltd., Richmond, British Columbia.

The Bible version used in this publication is THE NEW KING JAMES VERSION. Copyright © 1979, 1980, 1982, 1990, Thomas Nelson, Inc., Publishers.

Library of Congress Cataloging-in-Publication Data
Ells, Alfred H.
  Family love : what we need, what we seek, what we must create / Alfred H. Ells.
        p.   cm.
    ISBN 0-8407-4559-1 (pbk.)
    1. Family—Psychological aspects.   2. Family—Religious life.   3. Parent and child.
4. Intergenerational relations.   5. Love.   I. Title.
HQ518.E435   1995
306.85—dc20   94-48153
                                                            CIP

Printed in the United States of America.

1 2 3 4 5 6 — 00 99 98 97 96 95

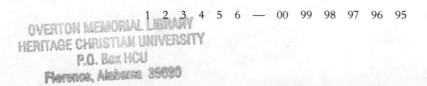

For Mel and Katie,
Matt and Andy,
and the
generations to come

CONTENTS

ACKNOWLEDGMENTS

Without Susan, my wife, this book would never have been. She has encouraged, challenged, and stirred me toward a deeper understanding of family. Her research, insight, and editorial support have been invaluable.

I also want to acknowledge Susan's sister, Patty Bilby Moore. She's been my faithful and gifted consultant, lending suggestion and direction to the project, making it truly a family effort.

And René Mummert, my secretary, deserves special thanks. She untiringly prepared the manuscript, always available and helpful.

Introduction

This is a book about how love works in families. It is important because how we give and get love in our families determines much of our future success or failure in relationships. Who we marry, how we love, and how we parent are all influenced by patterns of love.

As a marriage and family therapist, I have witnessed what the absence or presence of healthy love does to a family and its future generations. Most families don't have this conscious knowledge of how the family past has shaped current relationships, marriages, and children. In this book I want to share the insights I have learned from my own struggles and from the work I do in my family counseling practice and specialized Family Week programs. I want to offer you those understandings of relationships that will help transform your life and family—ones that will help you create new, healthier patterns of giving and getting love. These patterns will not only make family life more fulfilling for you but will also help your children avoid repeating your mistakes.

The stories I tell are ones of families and individuals I have worked with. Their names and identities have been changed and concealed as composites of several case histories. In their stories of pain and victory you will see how families like yours overcome the obstacles that diminish love while fashioning new ways to love. You will have the opportunity to resolve your family problems and re-create the healthy love that was lost or never known in the family experience. Join me in exploring how to create the family love we all seek and need.

PART 1

FROM GENERATION TO GENERATION

We are who we are because of our families. Nothing affects the way we think, feel, act, and react as much as the family, past and current. It is in the incubator of family life that both blessing and curse are pronounced on future generations.

CHAPTER 1

The Truth
About Family

The apple doesn't fall far from the tree.
—Italian proverb

Kelly's Story

Sharon Carpenter and her aerospace engineer husband, Philip, attended one of our weeklong family therapy programs. Sharon's teenage daughter, Kelly, a child of a previous marriage, was causing considerable trouble and concern. In an attempt to understand and change Kelly's behavior, the Carpenters came for Family Week. Kelly's biological father, Ed McGuire, came as well.

During Family Week, five or six families meet together in groups to share their concerns and problems and learn from the therapist and each other. During the early part of the week, it was Sharon's turn to tell her family's story, as Ed, her ex-husband, listened reluctantly.

3

"When her girlfriend's mother called, I thought it was an error. I never dreamed Kelly would do such a thing!" Sharon exclaimed. "She had always been such a good kid. But she lied to us. She was sneaking out of the house every time she got a chance. We confronted her, and she still lied. She said her girlfriend's mother must have mistaken her for a girl named Shelly. I took her word for it and called her girlfriend's mother back. She said she would investigate. You can imagine how horrified I was when she reported there was no doubt about it. Kelly and her girlfriend had been sneaking out of the house to meet boys. Why would Kelly do such a thing? I'm still so hurt I can hardly stand to look at her. Just when things were starting to straighten out, this has to happen. It seems like my life is just one big problem after another."

Sharon explained how difficult it was to accept and deal with her fifteen-year-old daughter's obsession with boys. In a two-month period Kelly had left the house without permission over a dozen times. Each time she and her girlfriend had rendezvoused with a group of boys from school. Sharon's hurt and puzzlement were compounded by the worry that Kelly's eleven-year-old sister might be influenced by Kelly's behavior.

In the years following her divorce, Sharon was a single mother and sole provider for Kelly and her sister Jennifer. She was so stressed from work, school, and family responsibilities that she frequently raged when she had a bad day and the girls irritated her. In her loneliness she drew Kelly close to her for companionship.

"She was my best friend for so long. I could always count on her to take care of her sister and help me with the house. We spent a lot of time together talking," Sharon said.

When Philip showed interest in her at work, she was wary at first, not wanting to involve herself in another failed relationship. But Philip pursued and she relented. He was stable and steady, offering her the security and relief from pressure she craved. They were married last Christmas—just a few months before Kelly's problem surfaced.

Family life for Kelly was a roller coaster of emotions, feeling close and loved by Sharon at one moment, and hurt and rejected by her anger the next. Sharon's temper lessened with Philip's presence, but her attentiveness also decreased. Kelly had a need for her mom's acceptance, attention, and love but felt rejected because her mom now gave her time to Philip. The answer to her loneliness and hunger for love was being met by the attention of boys. Filling her needs this way also brought her to the brink of sexual experimentation. One of the boys had pressured her for sex, and she had almost given in to get the love she craved.

Neither Kelly nor her parents realized the full impact of her family legacy on Kelly's current behavior. She was unwittingly responding to long-standing family patterns of imperfect love and mismanaged closeness—ways of getting and giving love that predictably influenced her to seek out love in wrong ways. As our Family Week progressed, the controlling patterns of deficient love became clearer.

Unknown to all of us, Sharon Carpenter had been harboring a secret all week that she was longing to let out. Toward the close of the week, she became more and more anxious. Finally, she blurted out, "Shouldn't Kelly know she's not the only one in the family with a problem? I can't just sit here and pretend any longer. I don't think Kelly's problems are all because of the mistakes she, Philip, or I made. Ed is also to blame."

The room was silent. Everyone turned to look at her ex, Ed McGuire. Sharon and Ed had been married ten years, and they divorced when Kelly was five years old. Ed had been a surprise guest at Family Week. Though he was invited, we were worried he would refuse to come. He had shown little interest in Kelly's life over the years and had rarely contacted his daughter.

Ed turned scarlet with rage: "I knew you couldn't leave well enough alone. You just can't let go, can you? You have to stir up trouble and blame me just like you always did!"

He shook his head, angrily shoved his chair back, and left the room. We were all stunned by the interchange. It happened so quickly that no one was quite sure what to make of his reaction. Sharon was tense and afraid but still insistent: "I just couldn't sit here and let him get away with it."

"Get away with what?" I asked.

"I can't tell you," Sharon responded. "I promised Ed that if he came to Family Week, I would not talk about it with you or the other families." The rest of the group was silent, unsure of whether to press for disclosure of the secret or to let it alone. I wasn't sure what to do, either. Secrets are destructive to families, but pressing hard for their disclosure can make a bad situation worse. Fortunately, it was time for lunch. As they were leaving to eat, I encouraged the families to consider what they wanted to do with the issue when we returned.

"Someone wants to see you outside," the waitress whispered before I could take a bite out of my sandwich. I walked out the door and found Ed leaning against a tree and smoking a cigarette.

"I need to talk to you," he said in an agitated voice. "When I left, I swore I'd never come back, but after I got a cup of coffee and cooled off, I knew I had to stay. If not for Kelly's sake, at least for my own."

"Does this have to do with the secret?" I asked, motioning

Ed toward a nearby bench. Haltingly, he unfolded his story. Ten years ago he had molested Sharon's thirteen-year-old niece. When Sharon confronted him about it, he refused to admit the truth, accusing her niece of lying and trying to get him in trouble. The blowup prompted Sharon to file for divorce. In his shame and fear Ed quickly left town, rarely making contact with his two daughters over the following years.

Ed continued, "I never did it again. I felt so terrible about what I had done that it was years before I could forgive myself. I wondered how I could have been so sick as to molest a young girl. I even thought about suicide. I swear to you I have never touched another girl in the last ten years. I was only twenty-eight at the time and very foolish. Believe me, I've punished myself a hundred times over for doing it. I can't bear to have Sharon rub it in."

As Ed and I talked, he disclosed more of his past. He had been a victim of someone in his own family, molested by a relative at eleven years of age. I encouraged Ed to come back to the group and share what he told me.

When the session resumed that afternoon, Ed asked if he could talk first. He nervously shared his wrongdoing with Sharon's niece and his secret from his childhood. Ed confessed that he had never wanted to neglect his children, and that he had been running away from his fear and guilt. His childhood molestation had contributed to his violation of Sharon's niece. His family legacy of mismanaged sexuality had cost him a marriage and Kelly a father's love.

Moved by his honesty, Sharon allowed her anger to subside. "I've never been able to forgive you for what you did," Sharon responded. "I could never understand why you did it and then lied about it. You made my niece look like the liar, and she was only the innocent victim of your lust. It's still going to be hard for me to forgive you. But it has helped me to understand that you did it because of what happened to you. I am willing to work toward forgiving you . . . especially if you will be honest and face your problem. I've been afraid to trust you with the girls because of what you did."

Ed's willingness to face his hurtful past offered Sharon, Philip, Kelly, and himself the hope of a new beginning. It was a large step toward removing the barriers between them, giving the family an opportunity to create new and healthier ways of relating in the present, ways that could help Kelly escape her unhealthy way of seeking love.

In the closing session Ed, looking steadily into her eyes, shared his heart with Kelly: "Honey, I've never been a father to you. But now that my secret is out in the open I want to help you. Relationship problems have been in our family for generations, and you are going to have to learn to overcome them like I've had to. I don't want you to make the same mistakes I have made. My problem ruined our family. I don't want to see you ruin your life. I will help you any way I can."

The unhealthy family patterns were being challenged and new ones created.

Family Problems

The Carpenter family is not alone in its need for change. Today's families are in crisis. The media constantly herald the difficulties of single-parent homes, blended families, couples in conflict, and the breakdown of traditional family values. Problems like Kelly's are not rare exceptions any longer; neither is Sharon's struggle to find security and fulfillment for herself and her family. Drugs, violence, financial hardship, teenage rebellion, alcoholism, sexual abuse, and moral erosion are just a few of the enormous strains on family life, causing fractured and strife-filled relationships. When people experience problems, their relationships suffer.

Problems, people, and relationships are intertwined. The rapid-fire pace of change in American family life is testimony to this fact. Divorce rates skyrocketed in the 1960s and 1970s, giving rise to a radical shift in family life. There are now more single-parent households and blended families than traditional ones. Today, one in four Americans lives alone, and many are afraid to marry, citing the high failure rate. The changes have created a ripple effect of greater financial and relational problems. Studies suggest that a child raised in a single-parent home is more likely to live in poverty and is thirteen times more likely to be abused than one from a traditional, intact family. Children in blended families are more likely to have two working parents and are forty times more likely to suffer abuse. More than ever before there is a need for each of us to understand how to keep our marriages and families together and create the love we all need and seek.

The problems we experience today are tied to the past— the family past. Nothing affects the way we think, feel, act, and react as much as our families do. To a great extent we are who we are because of our families of origin. The problems and negative patterns of behavior we experience today are directly related to who raised us and how we were raised. There is an old saying, "The apple doesn't fall far from the tree." In our high-tech age, however, we have lost sight of much of its wisdom. Because we are products of our genetics and our environment, family is the single greatest determiner of who we are, how we act, and what we believe. We will, in many ways, be like our parents. We will act as they do and even repeat many of the same mistakes they made. Our patterns of behavior and styles of relationship will be affected greatly by our relationships with them. *Issues such as who we marry, why we love, and how we parent will be influenced by our families of origin.*

Our family legacies are powerful shapers of our destinies. We learn the fundamentals of life within our families. The family is the link with the past and the bridge to the future. It's through our family relationships we learn how to relate to others and ourselves. Out of our family life we develop the patterns of giving, caring, and loving that make up our framework of love in relationships. Here is a key truth that few people truly understand: most relationship problems stem from unquenched family love hungers—deep, unfilled needs to receive and give love that come from the family past. Understanding how a family creates or satisfies each member's love hunger reveals the hidden cause of many family problems. The ensuing chapters will show how this dynamic works and what you can do to re-create healthy patterns of loving and giving—ones that satisfy and fulfill the love hunger in healthy ways. By re-creating these healthy patterns, of course, you are also re-creating family. The patterns of getting and giving love in a family are the basic shapers of family life. But first we must explore how families shape the need for love and the ways in which it is sought.

Needing and Seeking Love

The radical shift of family life in recent years has produced an even greater need for healthy family love. Single-parent homes place extraordinary requirements on one parent to be everything a child needs. Blended families have formidable obstacles to overcome in forging healthy closeness, respect, and love among all the members. Traditional, intact families are no exception. It takes a lot of love, patience, and understanding to make families work. The patterns of love in a family are the glue holding the family together. When the love is deficient, the family will suffer.

I believe the answer to most family problems lies mainly within the way families get and give love. Within each family, whether a single-parent, blended, or traditional one, the fundamental felt need is for love and closeness. When problems surface, the bonds of love are challenged. Where closeness is lacking, there is no strength to face the world and its pressures. And when love is not abundantly offered within the family, its members seek it elsewhere in unhealthy ways. How a family structures itself to give and receive love can mean the difference between fulfillment or failure in the family and the individual's life.

In every person there is a reference base for understanding love. Everyone has certain ideas about what it is like to give love and what it is like to receive it. These beliefs, largely developed in the family, are the *framework of love*. They result in both direct and indirect expressions of love. Some individuals have great difficulty saying, "I love you," directly because no one ever said it to them when they were children. Some families taught that money and gifts, not hugs and kisses, were the acceptable way to express love. Indirect expressions of love, like the direct ones, are powerful shapers of how we give and get love.

Kelly felt loved when her mother spent time with her, when she shared with Kelly her innermost thoughts and feelings. She also felt cared for when Mom sat on the couch next to her rubbing her back and stroking her arm with featherlight touches. Kelly's framework of love was sensual, intimate

—connected only with femininity because she lacked close relationship with her dad or any other older male.

Kelly's deep need for love was also an issue. Along with our framework of love, which deals with *how* we get and give love, is our need for love, which is a matter of the intensity or craving we have for love. Our families also dictate how much love we need. Every family's obligation is to raise children to become responsible, contributing adult members of society. To do so requires a special combination of love and discipline. Every child has deep needs for belonging, acceptance, approval, attention, and affection. When these needs are not fully met by the parents, the child will develop a *love hunger,* a deep need for the love, acceptance, or attention never fully received in childhood. Needs are vacuums seeking to be filled. The extent of love hunger from childhood will affect how desperately we need relationships. It will also influence our choice of spouses and friends.

Kelly suffered from a deep love hunger due to her dad's absence and her mom's come close–stay away style. Aside from Mom's occasional flurries of intimacy toward her, she felt lonely and rejected. Her lack of a steady supply of acceptance, approval, and belonging created a hungry longing for it. When a young girl doesn't feel loved, she secretly fears that it is because she isn't lovable. Consequently, Kelly did not feel good about herself.

The attitudes you develop about yourself through interactions with your parents become the basis of your self-worth and self-image. Psychologists call this *self-concept,* the sum total of all your thoughts, beliefs, images, and perceptions about yourself. Self-concept reflects the way you value yourself and understand yourself. The way you were treated by your family had everything to do with how you ended up feeling about yourself. If one or both parents were very critical, their criticism could make you critical of yourself. A nurturing family, on the other hand, kept building a sense of confidence and self-worth in you.

Kelly's mother, Sharon, came from an unhealthy home where her father was an alcoholic binger. Sharon's mom would draw her close and dote on her when Dad was on a spree, but would criticize and distance herself from Sharon at other times. Both the push-pull pattern and the criticism Sharon communicated to Kelly were repeats of her family past. They made Kelly doubt herself. Her father's absence and rejection further lowered her self-esteem. She wondered if there was something the matter with her that caused her dad to contact her so rarely and her mom to come so close and then push her away. She felt unsure of herself and desperately wanted a boyfriend to love her. Because her parents didn't seem to value her much, she didn't think that any boy would want her either.

Kelly responded in an unhealthy manner to her family's deficient styles of giving love by sneaking out to meet boys. Her rebellion only made her problems of low self-worth and love hunger worse. Beneath her pretty features was a wounded heart crying out for the caring it had never fully received. Kelly needed the healthy love and honesty that only her family could bring. Their willingness to reevaluate and change their unhealthy patterns was the beginning of change for Kelly.

The family, more than any other factor outside ourselves, will determine who we are and how we behave. This is especially true with our problems in life and in relationships. Marriage choices, sexual problems, depression, codependency, alcoholism, eating disorders, and teenage rebellion have everything to do with the family past. The influences that shaped our lives also helped create our problems. Facing the family past is a major key to change. It offers us the hope of analyzing what went wrong and developing a plan for change. Understanding the family past gives insight into the steps we can take to intervene, break the unhealthy behavior patterns, and create new ways of getting and giving love. But we must be careful how we approach dealing with the family past.

The Two Extremes

Most people have difficulty admitting their faults and imperfections. It is even harder to face the reality of an imperfect family. When faced with the truth about families of origin, people may go to one of two extremes. One extreme is to excuse one's family failings by saying, "They did the best they could," and never face the issues. The other extreme is to place blame. Kelly had a difficult time believing that her family could have anything to do with her problem. Sharon, on the other hand, was all too willing to blame everything on Ed.

When we are in the grip of an attitude of unhealthy blame, we do not see matters in an unbiased, realistic context. We attempt to assign fault in a judgmental way. This attitude has a punishing flavor to it. It focuses on the past, stuck in thinking how bad things were instead of thinking of the future and what needs to change. Blame needs to be replaced with ownership of our faults and a willingness to change. Each of us needs to clarify how we have contributed to the problem and how we can modify future behavior for the better. Ownership is a necessary step toward healing, a supportive uncovering of truth, not a negative accusation of fault. Without taking responsibility for our past actions, we remain stuck in bitterness and weakness. Unhealthy blame, by pointing the spotlight on someone else, provides an excuse for avoiding the responsibility to face our contributions and change.

Denial, however, can be just as dangerous, tending to soothe our senses and keep us in bondage. We will keep repeating the unconscious negative patterns and weaknesses of the family unless we face them fully and commit to resolving them. The real roots of denial are fear and self-protection. We say we do not want to hurt our parents, but underneath we are afraid they will hurt us, rejecting us if we confront them with the truth. What we protect in others is frequently what we protect in ourselves. Our fear of their rejection or loss of their admiration or love causes us to balk at examining the truth. Our love hunger doesn't want to risk their rejection.

The Family Quilt

The understanding that every family is imperfect needs to be balanced by the realization that every family is also wonderfully unique and complex. Like the squares of a fascinating quilt constructed over the generations, family members contribute in a special way to its distinctiveness. Some squares are fashioned with care and skill and strengthen the whole for years to come. Others are flawed or funny or poignant. Some families are like patchwork, hectic and chaotic; others are carefully patterned from generation to generation.

It is a wonderful thing to value your family heritage. It is also important to step back from it and get an overview of where it has come from and where it is going. How is the pattern developing in your family? Where does it need to be strengthened, changed, appreciated, and treasured? Can you look at it realistically, accepting both the pain and the joy it has brought you? You are challenged to draw from the family's strengths, remedy its faults, and contribute your unique work to its artistry.

The truth is that there are no perfect families. Families are made up of people, and people are imperfect. A full acceptance of the strengths and the problems, the joy and the pain, the benefits and the drawbacks of our families is a healthy starting place for life and growth. The right question is not "Who is to blame?" but "What is God showing me about my need to grow through my family legacy?" We have the opportunity, if we will seize it, to eliminate our unhealthy family patterns and create new and healthier ways of loving, giving, and caring.

We have seen that the patterns of the past have a powerful influence on the problems of the present. Creating new and healthier family patterns of love begins with recognition and ownership of unhealthy ones. As we look back at the past to uncover root problems, we must avoid the pitfalls of denial and blame, embracing the entire family history as we seek to alter the future.

As we shall see in the following chapter, the journey toward healthy family love begins with the generations of family before us. The love patterns of the past create the "I care" messages of today, foreshadowing fulfillment or failure.

CHAPTER 2

Passing On Healthy Love Patterns

Family is our link with the past and our bridge to the future.

—Alex Haley

When you hear the words *generational strongholds,* you may envision mighty bastions that have withstood the attacks of enemies for generations and are still standing. English castles, Moorish citadels, and Spanish fortresses all come to mind. These powerful strongholds took many years to build, some even generations.

Personal, relational, and familial problems can also be thought of as mighty fortresses that withstand change. Ongoing weaknesses or deficient love patterns that gain a firm hold on our lives become powerful controlling influences that resist our ability to conquer them. Most of us don't realize that these strongholds are generational. That is, they were born in the incubator of family life, possibly generations before us, and are still living out their power in our lives today. One way we can recognize this phenomenon is by seeing individuals repeat family mistakes or hurtful patterns.

In fact, we can find a vivid example in the Bible of a family that repeated its mistakes. The hurtful family pattern began with a committed family man named Abraham who was married to a beautiful woman, Sarah.

We are told that in Abraham's early years he lied about his beautiful wife, Sarah, calling her his sister. They were traveling in a foreign land, and he wanted to avoid the possibility of being harmed by the men of that land who may have wanted Sarah for her beauty. A later story recounts how his son of promise, Isaac, lied to the men of Gerar. Isaac told them that his beautiful wife, Rebekah, was *his* sister because he feared they might kill him to have her! Abraham's weakness of character was also displayed in his son. The family exhibited a sort of generational cowardliness—an attitude of lack of trust and faith in God to protect them if they told the truth. The two instances of lying could represent a generational stronghold of fear and lying, demonstrating how the mistakes of the father are repeated by the son.

Other Family Strongholds

Other strongholds, such as anger, rage, fear, sexual problems, depression, abuse, self-pity, and so forth, also run in families. My family had serious problems with anger. My dad's father was an angry man who came from a rough-and-tumble mining town. Grandpa would bring a shotgun to the dinner table and use it to threaten all twelve of his children if they weren't orderly and quiet. Dad and his brothers registered the results of their father's unbridled anger, carrying the curse of it throughout their lives. One brother went to prison for killing his wife, another was a boxing champion in the navy, and two others spent more than one night in jail for drunkenness and fighting. My dad had a violent temper and was physically and verbally abusive when angry. We all tiptoed around Dad, not wanting to get too close and trigger his temper. Living in our house required navigating the minefields of Dad's anger. When he wasn't angry, he was jovial, fun loving, and great to be with. This is true of many men and women who rage. They can be the nicest people you have ever met—unless you cross the invisible line where their anger explodes.

I can remember sitting on the back steps of our house after one of Dad's rages. Hot tears were rolling down my cheeks, and I felt hurt, angry, and confused. I vowed I would never treat my wife or children the way he treated his. But the anger my father inherited from my grandfather was passed on to me. Even though I was afraid of anger, I still got angry in the only way I knew how—I raged. I exploded with angry accusations and cursing. Then in five minutes I was over it. I had gotten it all out of my system and felt good again, but my wife, Susan, was still reeling from my outburst.

Susan came from a family where anger was expressed differently. People in her family rarely yelled, cursed, or lost their tempers. They handled their anger primarily through withdrawal and the cold shoulder treatment. This type of anger is called *passive-aggressive,* and it is fueled by internal hostility and self-pity. It is a way of being angry and punishing others without being outwardly aggressive. Self-pity and the excuse that "I am hurt" become smoke screens for aggression. Susan's silent treatment would eventually anger me further and make me explode again. In retribution she would add on three more days of the silent treatment.

Our individual strongholds of anger produced an unhealthy pattern of conflict and offense between us. When individual strongholds go unchallenged in us, they result in patterns of interactions with others that are hurtful, preventing us from giving or getting love. The destructive pattern of action and reaction continued until we both realized that we were really dealing with strongholds in ourselves and each other. Our anger was creating the type of family we didn't plan to have or want. The unhealthy pattern was in control; we weren't.

Unhealthy Patterns

Negative relationship patterns are common to many marriages and families. Though frustrating and painful to those involved, the patterns don't affect only them—they are also passed on to their children and children's children. Once again, the Bible story of Abraham and his family illustrates that behaviors and unhealthy relationship patterns can be passed on from generation to generation. Favoritism is one such negative pattern.

The preference of one child over another is a reflection of improper bonding within the family. Bonding in families is the emotional connection that keeps us together. When favoritism exists, there is a favored attachment toward one child that creates unfair and unhealthy patterns of love. The favoritism will cause a love hunger in the one not favored and promote unrealistic expectations of love in the one favored. These hurtful relationship patterns have a way of repeating themselves because families and individuals do not acknowledge their presence and set up a plan for change. During a family camp, a colleague, Dave Stoop, shared the following analysis of our Old Testament friend Abraham and his family.

As you may recall, Abraham and Sarah were promised a son by God, but because of Sarah's pressure and his impatience, Abraham fathered a son, Ishmael, by Sarah's maid. When Sarah finally bore Isaac, Abraham banished Ishmael and favored Isaac, the child God had promised him through Sarah. Isaac grew up and married Rebekah and in turn favored his son Esau, while Rebekah favored their other son, Jacob. When Jacob married, he favored his son Joseph over Joseph's brothers. In each case the pattern of favoritism caused deep wounds, family disintegration, and continuing problems. Ishmael was ostracized all his life, Jacob had to flee his brother for fear of his life, and Joseph was sold into slavery by his brothers.

Unhealthy love patterns always evoke reactions from others that result in further pain. There is a ripple effect that continues to spread the problem to others. As we see in Abraham's family, hurtful patterns perpetuate themselves over generations unless something is done to change them.

Patterns of Love

A love pattern is a recurring set of behaviors that you exhibit when giving or getting love. It's basically how you "do" love. A love pattern comes from your family and is passed on to future generations. How you interact with Mom, Dad, brothers, sisters, and others determines how you relate to your spouse and children. As you shall see in following chapters, your closeness or distance to your family caretakers and loved ones produces the love patterns you adopt for life.

The bonding patterns of family life influence the ways you

will get and give the love you need in adulthood. These patterns become the measure of closeness you incorporate into your family dream for the future. They influence your choice of a spouse, the success of your marriage, and the way you parent your children.

Research has shown that most of the personal and relational problems many of us experience are caused by the inability to bond in healthy ways. We can share love when we draw close to each other, but we feel rejection when we are distant. This makes the way in which members of a family bond to each other the most powerful shaping force of family life.

To formulate healthy family dreams and legacies for our children, we must examine our bonding patterns and how we get and give love. Codependent and counterdependent ways of getting and giving love are the most common unhealthy bonding or love patterns. Understanding how these patterns work offers insight for improving the family legacy of love. When the codependent or counterdependent love patterns are identified and challenged, healthy love and connection can begin—not only for us but also for future generations.

Codependent Love Patterns

One-way or one-sided relationships are very common. One person in the relationship seems to give, care, or love more than the other. This pattern is found in work relationships, marriage, parent-child relationships, and even churches. In *One-Way Relationships: When You Love Them More Than They Love You,* I explained how a wounded heart's cry for love is at the core of one-sided relationships. Love that was never received as a child, or the overprotective love of childhood that we want to re-create as adults, prompts us to give love in order to receive it. We want someone to love us as we love; therefore, we give or care much more than the other person does. We desire the rich feelings of oneness, intimacy, and security that were either missing in our childhood or present in such abundance that adult life without them leaves a gaping hole. People with wounded hearts who have not resolved the love hunger stemming from childhood continually seek one-sided relationships. They give because they want to get. What they offer is what they so desperately need. This pattern of lopsided caring and one-way loving is called *codependence*.

Growing up in my family, I developed codependent patterns of loving, caring, and giving in relationships. Dad's rageful anger scared me, making it safer to tiptoe around him and others, trying extra hard to please to make sure no one got mad at me. His unconquered stronghold of anger and rage provoked unhealthy patterns in me. I always tried to make others happy by avoiding conflict or anything that might cause them to reject me. I also developed codependent patterns of loving due to Mother's unfulfilled need for closeness in her relationship with Dad. Their marital conflicts caused her to draw me close, too close, and confide in me about their problems. My response was to try to please my mother to keep her from being as disappointed in me as she had been in Dad.

My pattern of doing everything I could to please my wife, Susan, was a direct result of my relationship with my family. I would promise Susan anything she wanted to keep her from being disappointed in me. Obviously, I was unable to always follow through on what I promised and what she wanted me to be, thus making things worse between us instead of better. My unhealthy response was to redouble my efforts at pleasing. I never realized how I was setting myself and the relationship up for failure. The family we were creating together (Susan and I and the children) was being destroyed by the pattern of loving we had learned from our families.

Counterdependent Love Patterns

Another unhealthy love pattern is called *counterdependence* —the opposite of codependence. This pattern of relating can be seen in individuals who have difficulty with closeness, intimacy, and sharing. Susan's style of relating was at times very counterdependent. She expected me to share my heart and make the extra effort to keep the relationship working between us, yet she reserved the right to withdraw and not contribute to the marriage equally.

Counterdependent people require relationship on their terms. Love hunger prompts them to pursue bonds with others but only on their own terms. They want to be on the receiving end of the relationship, prizing their independence and fearing vulnerability.

Susan's family past precipitated her counterdependence. Her mother and father were not close to her. Susan's dad came from a family that required high achievement and success in order to be accepted. His pursuit of acceptance resulted in work habits that rarely allowed him to spend quality time parenting his children. His lack of involvement produced a deep love hunger in Susan.

Susan and her mom were also too loosely connected. Because she was overburdened by having to assume full responsibility for the children, her mom was often critical of Susan. To satisfy her resulting love hunger, Susan became very close to her younger sister Patty, who felt sorry for her and took care of her emotionally. Susan's love hunger developed into a caretaking relationship between her and her sister, allowing Patty to take too much responsibility for soothing her older sister's wounds. The result of Susan's family legacy was a counterdependent style of relating that hindered her ability to remain intimate and equally responsible in our marriage. She depended too much on me to take care of her.

Strongholds of anger, fear, and wrong bonding result in unhealthy patterns in marriage and family life. Negative patterns become so powerful that they overshadow healthy patterns of love. Recognizing that our codependent and counterdependent love patterns were not working for either of us led to our commitment to change. Susan and I resolved to create a family, a lifestyle, that was new—a re-creation.

I stepped back into my past and resolved the wounds of my childhood and the ways my family expressed anger. Susan did the same. We committed to learn new and better ways of expressing love to each other. As the upcoming chapters reveal, we negotiated new ways of managing closeness and resolving conflict. The steps we took brought relief and helped us fashion a new dream of healthy closeness and love. For some time afterward we occasionally slipped into our old patterns but not as often or as long as before. When we did, we stopped ourselves, asked forgiveness of each other, and tried again. Recognizing, admitting to, and working toward change stop the unhealthy patterns and give opportunity for creating new ones. These steps toward change also allow the healthy patterns of giving and getting love to once again surface and prevail. Family re-creation frees us from hurtful strongholds while impelling us to adopt healthy love patterns.

Creating Healthy Love Patterns

Healthy families have certain characteristics and patterns of relationship that minimize strongholds and maximize the healthy growth of the individual. Not only should we work toward eliminating the unhealthy codependent and counter-dependent patterns, but we should preserve and encourage the healthy ones. Kindness, tenderness, and caring are assets to any relationship. Honesty, transparency, and the ability to admit wrongdoing are also helpful. These and other qualities are part of what healthy love patterns are all about. Positive demonstrations of love are appropriately titled "I care" messages. To build healthy generational patterns of love, positive "I care" behaviors must be incorporated into the fabric of family life and relationship.

Families use two types of "I care" messages to verbally and nonverbally communicate affection and caring: (1) *direct* means and (2) *indirect* means. The direct ways of saying "I care" do not need a lot of interpretation. The act itself is a clear message of love that requires no interpretation—the sender's intent is understood. Examples of direct ways of saying "I care" include the following:

- Conveying a direct verbal message (for example, saying, "I love you")

- Giving appropriate and frequent touches, such as hugs, pats, and kisses

- Actively listening to another person speaking

- Displaying affection in positive ways (for example, smiling at another, reaching toward someone, or facing another)

- Being sexually intimate

- Disclosing yourself (for example, telling another what is in your heart by sharing your thoughts, feelings, dreams, and desires)

- Sharing your secrets with another person

The direct "I care" behaviors are positive ones that, when practiced on a routine basis, develop healthy patterns of love. The following indirect ones are also important ways to show love:

- Bestowing gifts, such as flowers, cards, or money

- Entertaining or cooking for others

- Spending time together or providing another easy access to you (for example, being willing for your spouse to interrupt a business meeting to get in touch with you)

- Playing with another (for example, boating, fishing, hiking, shopping, etc.)

- Doing favors for or providing a service to another (for example, serving breakfast in bed, running an errand, or giving a back rub)

Both direct and indirect ways of saying "I care" are important. A family needs both kinds liberally sprinkled throughout interactions. However, the direct ones are more valuable than the indirect ones. Research indicates families with emotionally disturbed children tended to overuse the indirect ones and underuse the direct. The indirect means often require interpretation.

Close families demand large amounts of affection displayed regularly. Families with little closeness may not provide enough affection for certain members. The exchange of clear, mutually agreed upon "I care" messages significantly affects the level of bonding and intimacy attained by family members. When bonding and intimacy are present, we not only *know* we are loved, we *feel* the love. This is the importance of building positive "I care" behaviors into our family relationships of love. They make us feel loved and cared for. The positive patterns of love encourage our self-worth and teach us how to relate intimately and appropriately with others.

An exercise that many families have found helpful in developing new patterns of love is to use these "I care" messages to interview each family member, asking which ones are preferred and how often they are desired. The family members then practice one of the identified behaviors each day for a week, rotating to a new one the following week. Each person has an opportunity to both give and get love in new, healthy ways.

Family Blessing

As I have mentioned before, our families can both bless us and curse us. Whether they make our lives better or worse depends on what they do with their inherited weaknesses. Problems develop when generational patterns of deficient love, care, and concern are not examined and revised. Parents tend to avoid exposing their weaknesses, thinking that if their children don't know about them, they will not be affected. Yet strongholds always reveal themselves in the manner in which the parents live. The unwillingness to admit their presence is more a product of shame than of wisdom. Codependent and counterdependent patterns of unhealthy loving are products of the family past. They represent strongholds that have remained unchallenged or unconquered in ancestors. The unhealthy love patterns of parents have influenced the way in which they raised children and related to each other. The children are products of their weaknesses as well as their strengths.

However, unhealthy love patterns such as codependency and counterdependency can be changed. The sins of the fathers need not be visited on the children. We can break the control that generational strongholds have on our lives if we face ourselves and God with the truth. The unhealthy love patterns of Susan's family and mine were at the root of our relationship problems. (Unhealthy love patterns were also the cause of serious problems in Abraham's family.) Change came for us as we realized that both of us were creating a family life and environment that neither wanted. We both committed to learning more about how we had developed such destructive patterns and what we could do to change them. We were both deeply disappointed in the family life we had created. We wanted something new. The most helpful keys to change came from realizing that the seeds of our destructive love were sown in the love patterns of the family past and that we could therefore change them.

As we continue to examine the foundations of family life, the shaping influences and patterns will become clearer. We must remember that creating healthy family love begins with

- recognizing that we all have strongholds and understanding that they come from the family past.

- resisting the need to blame our spouses, parents, caretakers, or families rather than seeing what God is trying to show us about ourselves and our need to change.

- realizing that our patterns of love are the essence of what family life and family dreams are all about. They are possibly the most powerful legacy we pass on to our children and our children's children.

- adopting new "I care" messages to create needed patterns of healthy love and closeness.

In the next chapter we will examine more closely how love and bonding patterns shape who we become, why we have problems, and what we can do to re-create our family patterns of giving and getting love. We will examine the opposite family traits of being either too close or too distant in our relationships with each other.

HEALTHY FAMILY CLOSENESS

Family life is incredibly subtle and complex. Everything is tied to everything else, and it's very difficult to figure out what's going on and what needs to change. Patterns of closeness and distance are perhaps the most important ways of viewing the need for change in families. They control the way we give and get love.

CHAPTER 3

The Ties That Bind or Bless

"Hold me tight!" is the persistent human cry.
—Donald M. Joy

We all have a need to be attached to other people. The strength of attachments within a family is termed *cohesion* by family therapists. Cohesion is the tie that binds us together. Its presence or absence is the motivating power behind most family love patterns:

> My family are my best friends. My sisters and I talk daily on the phone, and I go by Mom and Dad's house probably every day. We always spend Sunday afternoons together, going to Mom's for dinner. We're very close and so are our children.

> After thirty-five years of marriage Mom and Dad seem to have an incredibly close relationship that I haven't seen in other couples. They often hold hands. They do everything

together. They just can't get enough of each other. They even sound alike and finish each other's sentences.

Emotional connectedness, or cohesion, is a foundational element of relationship. It is the glue that keeps us together, adding heartfelt warmth to our relationships. Without emotional closeness we remain isolated, hindered in our relationships and personal development. Closeness within a family has always been a desired characteristic. Its presence in marriage brings the enriching intimacy and belongingness the inner being craves.

Child development specialists tell us that this need for attachment is a natural part of our makeup. We are social beings. Deep within every child is the need to be intimately connected to a caretaker. While in the womb, the developing child does not realize separateness from Mom. Even after birth, the growing infant intimately attaches to Mom, always wanting to be held or suckled. For healthy development to take place, the young child must be emotionally close or bonded. This closeness opens the person's developing inner being to life. A child must feel safe before taking the risk to explore the world.

Bonding lays the foundation for later trust, self-awareness, and sensitivity to others. It allows the parent to imprint the child with values, understanding, and healthy perceptions of the world. This mysterious quality of connectedness brings an inner feeling of peace, assurance, and well-being to the child. It makes the child feel secure and unafraid, and it is therefore a most powerful shaping influence. Its absence can cause deep woundedness, loneliness, and a tormenting love hunger.

Closeness Mishandled

Because cohesion is essential to family life, too much or too little of it can cause personal, familial, or marital problems. Relational or sex addictions, teenage rebellion, imbalanced marriages, divorce, loneliness, and depression can be symptoms of mishandled closeness. Behind the obvious problem is usually an empowering pattern of seeking or avoiding closeness.

Sex addicts, not knowing how to be intimate in healthy ways, are looking for love and closeness through sex. Rebellious teenagers defy rules because they aren't emotionally connected to healthy parental influence or, conversely, they are so close they feel smothered and rebel. Marriages suffer from hurtful, unbalanced patterns of loving, caring, or giving. One partner in the marriage wants to be close and does all the loving, giving, or pursuing, while the other person avoids, retreats, or refuses to give back. Depression, especially in women, can also be related to closeness issues. Many women feel lonely, alienated, unappreciated, unattractive, and unworthy because they are not closely bonded to their husbands. They've lost their hope of being loved and cared for in the way they have always desired, and they've lost faith in themselves.

Even problems with our parents stem from how close or distant we feel. Many adults have one-way relationships with their parents. They give, call, and extend themselves to their parents with little or no return. In other cases, the opposite is true. Parents reach out to adult children who rebuff them or who continually ask for money, favors, or gifts with no reciprocation. Sometimes parents and their adult children have only a superficial relationship that never progresses to the point of sharing hearts or true feelings. Somehow the closeness that would encourage the sharing is not there.

Our Family Roots

During Family Week, Susan and I frequently discuss with others the bonding patterns and legacies of closeness from our original families since they illustrate some typical mistakes. Our disclosure helps other families feel more comfortable with their shortcomings. Distortions of closeness are common to all families. It is rare that a marriage, and by extension a family, will have closeness and boundaries perfectly in balance. The patterns of closeness and bonding in Susan's and my families of origin had much to do with why we were attracted to each other, how our marriage has worked, and what problems we and our children have experienced.

With so many kids in my family, it was hard for my parents to be equally close to us all. I was the second of eight children and closest to my mother. My dad favored a younger brother who had black hair and resembled him—that is, until my first sister was born. She also had black hair and was the daughter he always wanted. When my second sister was born, she was favored because she was a girl. Probably because of his upbringing, my father found it much easier to relate warmly to his daughters than to his sons.

Mom remembers being close to my first sister, so she got love and attention from both parents. However, my next younger brother never seemed close to either Dad or Mom. He was what is known as the forgotten or "lost" child in our family.

Closeness was a mixed bag in our family. Some of us were close to one parent while others were close to the other parent. We also had differing levels of closeness between brothers and sisters. And our family patterns of closeness affected our later lives. For me, the relationship of closeness with my mom both blessed me and hurt me. I prized the intimate times of sharing with her. Our closeness made me feel loved, accepted, and appreciated. She and I were the best of friends, sharing thoughts, feelings, and dreams. She valued my opinion and lavished me with attention and affection. I flourished in the spotlight of her attentiveness.

But I was too close for too long. The pattern of being too intimately connected with Mom caused me problems later in life. That intense closeness was one of the major reasons why I chose Susan as a wife and why we had such difficulty in our marriage, parenting patterns, and family relationships. My mismanaged closeness with Mom created in me a deep need to be needed. Susan's legacy of deficient love readily attracted me, and my desire to comfort and care for her lured her to me. We were imbalanced in our relationship from the start because of our legacies of family closeness.

My relationship with my mom was the key influence in my one-sided patterns of loving, caring, and giving too much for all the wrong reasons. She and I were what family therapists call *enmeshed,* the state of being inappropriately close in a relationship. Enmeshment is hurtful to the child. It is an unhealthy closeness that is improper for the parent-child relationship and a child's developmental stage when it is necessary to create distance from the parent.

How Can Being Too Close Hurt Us?

When clients first hear that too much closeness can be harmful, they have mixed responses. Those who crave closeness are doubtful, and the ones who want distance are relieved. In either case, closeness and distance are sensitive subjects for many people. The closeness or lack of it that we have taken for granted in our family relationships needs careful examination. With too much closeness we can become stunted in our growth and addicted to unhealthy closeness in other relationships. With too little closeness we do not grow and will later live out lonely, disconnected lives. For two people to have a healthy relationship, their emotional closeness must be balanced with healthy independence. The family of origin's emotional bonding patterns will either encourage or hinder that needed balance. A legacy of unhealthy bonding patterns can create problems that will affect a wide range of issues from who we marry to how we parent and how we feel about ourselves.

Whitley Gardner came to me fearing that he was a hypochondriac. Raised as an only child, he had married Donna at a young age, shortly after the death of his mother. "When Mom died, I wanted to die, too," Whitley explained. "She and I were so close. It's been hard on me ever since. I still miss her, even though I have Donna and the kids. A psychologist told me that my health problems are due to my relationship with my mother. He said I still want someone to take care of me like she did. He may be right because Donna is always complaining that I can't do anything for myself. I guess it's true I never learned how to take care of myself."

There are several consequences to being raised in a situation where one is too emotionally bonded to a parent. Whitley was experiencing one of the most severe results of all, constant illness. Every flu bug, virus, and ailment found its way to Whitley.

"In the past year I can remember only one month that I was not sick," he declared. "I had a mysterious virus that the doctors never could diagnose, followed by strep throat, an intestinal blockage, and serious complications. I know Donna is getting awful tired of me being sick, but I can't do anything about it. I don't enjoy being sick, but my sicknesses are real."

Not every person with chronic illnesses comes from an enmeshed background. Since we are body, soul, and spirit, however, what affects us emotionally can also affect us physically. Whitley's physical problems were clearly connected to his emotional ones.

Whitley's mom had been overly bonded to Whitley since his dad died when Whitley was three years old. His dad had always been sickly and had finally succumbed to an undiagnosed malady. Whitley's mother was so afraid of losing Whitley that she overreacted by "protecting" him from every possible danger or disease. Whitley was constantly by his mother's side, and his mom did everything she could to make sure young Whitley stayed well. Because of the unhealthy enmeshment, the adult Whitley unconsciously felt he could not take care of himself.

When a parent and a child are too close, the parent will invariably overprotect the child, or the child will be overly concerned for the parent. This unhealthy cohesion makes for a protectionism that inhibits the child's healthy growth. I was overly concerned for my mother as a result of our enmeshment. Whitley's enmeshment caused his mother to be overly protective of him.

The challenge of parenting is the creation of responsible, mature, loving adults capable of fulfilling God's intentions for their lives. A dependent, intimately bonded child must come to the place of developing an inner sense of security, worth, and direction when grown. Whitley was unable to grow up and care for himself because he had learned a pattern of being cared for too much for too long. Fear kept his mother from encouraging Whitley's needed independence and self-care. I also remained too dependent on Mom's approval, love, and dreams for my life. Though seemingly independent on the exterior, inside I was living out her life, not mine. Being too close for too long had hindered each of us.

Healthy Closeness

Developmental psychologists have shown us that what is appropriate cohesion for one age range is inappropriate for another. If we graphed the way parent-child bonding should work over time, it might look like figure 3.1:

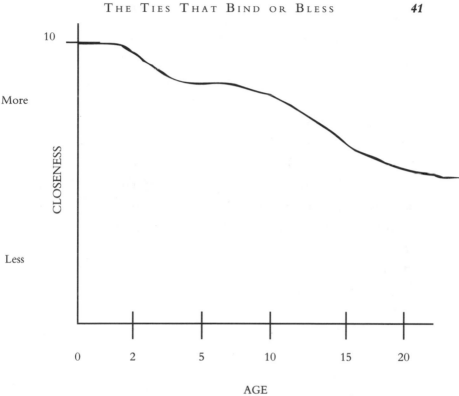

Figure 3.1. Appropriate Cohesion

As figure 3.1 indicates, we are intimately bonded to our caretakers at birth. By the time we reach late adolescence, we gradually become less dependent on others for the inner sense of well-being. To facilitate this transition, a parent must bond closely to the child at birth and then gradually transfer more and more responsibility for self onto the child as the child grows toward adulthood. If a parent remains too powerfully connected, intimate, or protective—and relies too much on the child to get needs for closeness met—the child will not mature. The child will not be able to separate from the parent and become an autonomous person. In this sense we all need a parentectomy. We may start life being intimately connected, loved, and protected by our parents, but we must grow toward internal direction, support, and decision making.

Emotional problems are created if we are too close for too long. As adults, we will experience fear, insecurity, self-centeredness, or love hunger. Whitley had an inordinate need to be taken care of. He remained dependent on others instead of growing up and developing healthy independence. He also unconsciously patterned his life after his father's. Whitley's dad was sickly and so was Whitley. Whitley's dad required someone to care for him and so did Whitley. For him, physical health was tied to emotional health. As he faced the unhealthy emotional bonding patterns of his past, physical wellness became possible.

Whitley Gardner's path to healing required him to first recognize how hurtful his family legacy of closeness had been for him. He thought the love he had received while growing up was healthy and desired. Counseling helped him realize that his dream and expectations of being cared for, loved, and overprotected were unrealistic results of mismanaged closeness. He grieved the loss of his dream and committed to learning new ways to love. But there was also an unexpected benefit to letting his dream go.

"I'm not as afraid as I used to be," he reported. "I was 'beset with fears' as my grandmother used to say. I was afraid to go to sleep at night or to drive in traffic or to meet new people. But since we've worked on letting go of my need to be taken care of, I'm less fearful, and I also trust God more."

Whitley's legacy of overprotectiveness was also one of fear. When a child is not encouraged to accept the challenges and difficulties of life, fear results. The parent's buffering of the child from problems and hurts creates doubts and fears in the child of adequacy to deal with life's many demands. Overprotectiveness puts the child at a disadvantage and hampers him from properly managing adult relationships.

Imbalanced Relationships and Roles

As mentioned earlier, codependent relationships are characterized by lopsided caring and one-way loving. One partner gives more in the relationship than the other.

Parental enmeshment is probably the single greatest cause of codependent patterns of relationship. When a parent remains too close for too long, the child either becomes too dependent, as Whitley did, or adopts a role of caretaker, as I did with my wife, Susan.

Families inadvertently create roles for each member. Roles are scripts or parts we play in the family dynamic. They are characteristic patterns of relating that become automatic. Our closeness or distance from our parents or caretakers encourages us to adopt a role in childhood that helps us get the needed attention, affection, or affirmation. Once established in childhood, the role becomes our unconscious script for adulthood, one that we are not even aware we are playing out. The role becomes an automatic response pattern that guides us whenever we want to get certain needs met. The most common roles in families are "hero," "scapegoat," "lost child," "mascot," and "caretaker."

In my family I was the "hero," the one who seemed to do everything right. I always made my parents proud of me, getting *A*'s in school, participating in sports, and winning good citizenship awards. Most families seem to have one child who makes the family proud of itself. This family hero enjoys the attention and affirmation the role brings but also pays a price for them. A hero is always expected to perform and never fail.

The hero is set up to meet everyone else's expectations but rarely to meet or even understand personal ones. My hero status came in great part from my enmeshment with Mom. I especially desired to perform well for her.

When one child in a family fulfills the role of hero, other children will play out the remaining typical family roles. My role of hero was in counterpoint to two of my brothers' roles of "scapegoat." The scapegoat stirs up trouble and always seems to be involved in some kind of unsanctioned behavior or naughtiness—as though the only way to get attention is by being the troublemaker or rebel. Though often appearing tough, the scapegoat is usually deeply wounded by the family dynamic and is rarely closely bonded to either parent. This lack of cohesion causes inner pain, and the scapegoat reacts to this wounding in angry or rebellious ways, setting oneself up for more rejection and reaction.

Frequently, the scapegoat bonds to another sibling to receive some validation and sense of belonging. Occasionally, the parents will view this as a threat to the sibling, thinking that the rebellion will rub off. More often, the sibling will act as a buffer between the parent and the rebellious brother or sister. The buffering sibling helps with communication and caring. At times, I acted as a buffer for both brothers. I nurtured and encouraged my younger brother and covered for my older brother with my parents.

My next younger brother was the "lost" or forgotten child. He never caused much of a ruckus and never drew much attention to himself. Most of the time he blended into the background of family life. The lost child will often spend time alone or with siblings, not becoming closely bonded to either parent. When grown, he may have problems connecting with other people, or he may develop a deep love hunger and need to reach out to others. My brother responded to his past in part by adopting friends who needed someone to belong to. It was as though his lack of intimate connectedness as a child caused him to reshape his legacy by re-creating his own family of lost children. That can be a healthy resolution for people who were raised as lost children. Friends can provide the love and connection they never had.

Some families have "mascots," jokers of the family who defuse family tensions through humor and also use humor to gain attention. Mascots are usually ambivalent about closeness. Their pattern of cohesion within the family has encouraged joking or cuteness as a way of connecting to others without being intimate. Mascots want to belong, and they desire the affirmation and validation that closeness brings; however, they are ambivalent about the vulnerability that true cohesion requires. Humor is a safe compromise.

Some female mascots use seductiveness as their tool for connection, as one young woman explained, "I got Dad's attention by being cute and sexy. He liked me to be around him, while Mom and I have never gotten along. The older I got, the better he and I connected. He could always count on me for a flirtatious comment or quick repartee. As I grew older I realized that most men liked me when I flirted with them." Playing the mascot role in a seductive manner can lead to an undesirable result. Men read the seductive playfulness as an invitation to sex and feel manipulated when sex is not forthcoming.

Many of us have tried playing the mascot or seduction role, hoping to meet our need for attention. My next youngest brother, the forgotten one, has also been a mascot of sorts. We can always count on him for a sarcastic comment, joke, or ribbing. Family members can, and sometimes do, play more than one role, but generally, one role will be more pronounced than another.

The most common result of being too close to a parent for too long is the "caretaking" role. When a child is enmeshed with a parent, the tendency is for the child to care too much for the parent. The child learns how to gain approval and attention primarily through meeting other people's needs. As well as being the hero, I was the caretaker in my family. I helped care for my grandfather, helping him out of bed and even feeding him. I also cared for a younger brother, taking him with me wherever I went. Many children help with grandparents or younger siblings in a healthy and positive way, but when being a caretaker becomes one's total definition of self, it becomes a problem.

Perhaps the most damaging caretaking I did in my family was in my relationship with Mom. Because of all the conflict in my parents' marriage, my mom confided in me, getting many of her intimacy and attention needs met through our relationship. We were the best of friends. Because of her problems with Dad, I always tried to make her feel better, siding with her and supporting her viewpoint. I became the caretaker for her feelings, and I tried to live out her dreams. She valued formal education and dreamed of attending college, but her marriage to Dad canceled her college plans. When I won a scholarship to the state university, I helped make her dream come true in my life, if not in her own.

I was both my mom's hero and emotional caretaker. Mom and I were too close for too long. The closeness created a powerful desire in me to please her and, by extension, others. I lived out other people's expectations, not defining my own. I didn't go to college for myself; I did it to make her and others proud of me.

My relationship with my mom and family left me with a deep need to be needed. Emotional caretakers know how to relate to others only through the role of being needed by another. The combination was a deadly setup for becoming involved with hurting or disappointed women. I wanted to care for them and make them feel better, be their hero, all the while denying my feelings and needs. Unknown to either Mom or me, the appreciated closeness had also been a stumbling block to my growth. What had previously seemed like enviable support and care was producing hurtful results. My closeness to Mom was related to my one-sided and codependent style of loving, caring, and giving too much to others for all the wrong reasons.

The answer to this emotional imbalance lies in great part with healing the effects of bonding patterns that were mismanaged by caretakers. Being too close to my mom for too long, I had difficulty detaching from the sense of security she gave me, her approval, and her dreams. Added to the situation was my detachment from my dad. When one parent is too close, the other will usually be too distant. Creating healthy love patterns required me to let go of Mom's dreams for me and search for my own. That came first as I recognized how my past patterns of closeness negatively affected my present. As my understanding grew, I saw that I needed to make a decision: Did I want to continue seeking something that was unhealthy and self-defeating, or was I willing to give up the dream and change?

A decision for change is always necessary, once you have recognized a problem. It's hard to let go of dreams and expectations of love—no matter how unhealthy or unrealistic they are. I had to choose to forsake the hero role, and I had to decide whether or not I was willing to let go of my deep desire for the excessive love of my past. I had to face my fear of not being loved in the future. God brought me to the place where the decision came easier than I had expected. My dreams and my patterns weren't working—no matter how hard I tried to make them. I grieved the loss of what couldn't be and forgave the wound caused by my dad's lack of love. My decision paved the way to healing and hope. It offered me the opportunity to create healthy love patterns for my life.

The Elusive Balance

As you can see, family closeness can either bind or bless. Achieving the proper balance of closeness and independence in family relationships is difficult. Most people struggle with these issues throughout life.

This struggle is complicated by the fact that our bonding needs change as we grow older. Early childhood requires more closeness; adolescence, a growing separateness and individuation. During adulthood, we should establish independence from parental influence while maintaining love, respect, and appreciation for our parents. This is the time that parents and children can truly become friends. With marriage and children, we begin anew the process of intimacy and bonding. The age-old cycle of attachment and release is reenacted. The family, God's profound and enduring plan for creation, continues in its paradoxical patchwork of delight and sorrow, forgiveness and struggle, comedy and drama, peace and perplexity. Our mission is to resist re-creating the negative patterns of relationship that keep us from getting and giving the love we so desperately need. It is also to reach out to God, asking Him to create in us new and healthy patterns of care, concern, and love.

In the following chapters, I will explain how enmeshment and its opposite, disengagement, relate to spouse selection, marriage, and parenting problems. I will also share how the unhealthy love patterns can be challenged and new ones created.

CHAPTER 4

We Were Never Close

Love is most intense where it is most practical, where the experiment in closeness is most intimate and daring.

—Mike Mason

I was never as close to Mom as my sister was, and I always felt hurt about it. I could see it even if she didn't, and my sister knew it, too. I thought there was something the matter with me, something she didn't like that made her choose my sister over me.

My dad and I never connected, even though I wanted to. I can't remember him ever saying that I did a good job or that he loved me. Mom told me that Dad was proud of my accomplishments, but you couldn't prove it by me. It's been hard since he died last May. There is so much I wish we could have talked about.

Mom and Dad never shared their inner thoughts or feelings with us kids. It's only recently that I have learned that I have feelings. Growing up in my home was like life in the army. You were expected to do what you were told and never complain. I felt lonely a lot of the time.

These people shared their experiences of growing up in families where they were not close to their parents. As we discussed in the last chapter, closeness is necessary for healthy emotional and spiritual growth; but many individuals come from families where they were never close to their mother, father, or anyone. This lack of connection has a negative effect on a person, even into adulthood.

Being too distant can be even more harmful than being too close. It creates inner strongholds of fear, insecurity, pain, or independence. It also gives rise to unhealthy family love. Individuals who come from backgrounds where emotional connection was lacking need to re-create their family love patterns. As we shall see, the lack of emotional closeness influences spouse selection, self-worth, and parenting styles. Re-creating family reconnects the love bonds that were lost or never experienced.

The term for being too distant from others is *disengagement*. Disengagement is the opposite of enmeshment. Some family members are comfortable with quite a bit of independence from each other. They have different interests and pursuits, yet still love and care for each other. Taking independence to an extreme, however, family members become disengaged. This type of relationship has more to do with the quality of emotional connections than with the number of shared activities. A disengaged family rarely shares on a feeling level. Each member is emotionally isolated—in a sense, hidden from the other members of the family. On the outside the family may appear to be functioning smoothly, but inside there are loneliness and separation.

Married couples can be disengaged as well. Partners live together and experience sexual intimacy, but they share little else. They may care for each other but not know how to convey it at a heart, or feeling, level. This inability to share feelings may come from the lack of closeness they experienced in childhood. It can also come from past wounds that made one or both individuals vow never to be vulnerable in love again.

In some cases, couples become disengaged over the years because it is easier to do than to wrestle with the issues and conflicts in the marriage. Uneasy with conflict, they manage to avoid unpleasant issues, but they also end up avoiding each other. This attitude may seem to be a safe way out of facing conflict, but the marriage is never able to realize its potential for intimacy, growth, companionship, and mutual comfort.

Patterns of disengagement, like those of enmeshment, come from the family past. How our mothers, fathers, or caretakers emotionally connected with us determines how we will love and relate to others. The patterns of healthy or unhealthy love start first with Mom.

Disengaged Moms

Most mothers eagerly await the arrival of their children and pour their lives into their cute and cuddly newborns. They stay up nights and spend hours feeding the babies, changing diapers, and saying, "Ga, ga, goo, goo." With all this focused energy and attention we assume that children and mothers will easily bond, and that problems with emotional attachment will rarely occur.

In spite of the love and attention, disengagement does happen between many mothers and children. The mother and the child do not bond closely. They do not emotionally and intimately connect with each other. It's as though the mother and the child get off to a wrong start from the beginning and never fully connect, or if they do bond closely at first, something happens to bring distance into the relationship.

I remember one mother who came to me as a client. She told me that her first child was difficult, colicky, and fussy all the time. As a young mother, she was inexperienced in handling her baby and felt resentful of his demands. Her second child, who came a year later, however, was a delight: a little girl who cooed and cuddled and easily bonded. She grew up being her mother's close friend while the older child grew more and more distant from the mother. While never desiring or intending it, the mother favored her second child over her first and never understood why her first child was so moody and such a loner. He registered the effects of never intimately connecting with anyone and of feeling rejected and resentful because of his sister's favored status.

Do mothers intentionally fail to bond with their children? I believe a lack of bonding between a mother and her child is rarely intentional. Most mothers who have difficulty bonding to their children do so because their parents never fully bonded to them, or the mother may prefer the characteristics of one child over another and not realize the impact on the child. Each person has preferences that affect bonding.

Still other mothers, however, experience problems that interfere with attachment. Any number of events, such as birth of another child, death of a close family member, or marital problems, can hinder the bonding process. Mom is too preoccupied, physically hampered, or emotionally distraught to give the time, love, patience, or attention needed. The child's needs compete with the mother's needs and lose. It is hard to give full love and devoted attention to a child when marital problems or crises are present. A compliant child who can be propped up in bed with a bottle may not receive the holding, touching, and playing needed to form a close bond.

It can also be very difficult to maintain an intimate bond with a child when a mother has to return to work in six weeks and cannot breast-feed or care for the child for the first two years when connection is established. Our modern lifestyle of busyness and two-parent incomes can compete with the necessary bonding cycle. When this crucial connectedness between mother and child is not fully developed in infancy and maintained at the appropriate level throughout childhood, the child pays the price.

Because Susan was not closely bonded with her mom, she struggled to bond with me in our marriage. She was unaccustomed to the feelings of shared closeness and vulnerability that marriage requires. When we were close, she could remain so only for short periods of time. She did not routinely experience the feelings of vulnerability as a baby, young child, or adolescent, making the feelings uncomfortable when practiced as an adult. Her lack of bonding with her mom also complicated her attempts to remain emotionally connected to our first child while she struggled with conflict in our marriage and worked full-time. However, because of my background of enmeshment, bonding with our daughter was easy for me. As a matter of fact, we became too close.

Enmeshed Dads

A common result of disengagement from the mother is enmeshment with the father. A child makes up for the lack of bonding with Mom by forming a close relationship with the other parent. Although at first this love connection is a life-saver for the child, in later years it can become a major stumbling block. The child can become too closely connected and too dependent on Dad. He will become overprotective of the child, even protecting the child from the mother. This reaction encourages the child to see Dad as the hero and Mom as the villain.

In our family I became too protective of my daughter, which made her relationship with Susan even more troubled and the disengagement more pronounced. Without realizing it I contributed to the disengagement until a good friend of ours pointed out my need to release my daughter to Susan and repent of being so protective. My gradual withdrawal of protectionism allowed Susan and our daughter to form a relationship without me in the middle. When a pattern of protectionism and disengagement becomes evident, the over-protective parent must relinquish control to allow the disengaged pair to attempt bonding.

Bonding can be accomplished if both, and especially the parent, work toward it. Our daughter was eleven when we saw our need to change. As I let go, Susan became more involved in our daughter's life. She planned activities they could do together that our daughter would like. She also worked on her criticalness and feelings of rejection. A vicious cycle of action and reaction broke as Susan resolved her feelings and I came to understand more about my unhealthy participation.

A pattern of disengagement or conflict between a mother and her child encourages Dad to become the buffer, who protects the child and the mother from each other. That was true not only of my family but also of Bert Cook's. He and his wife, Cheryl, came to my office for counseling because the conflict with their grown daughter Sadie was causing them to fight with each other.

Bert said, "When the two of them argue, nothing gets settled unless I get in the middle and help. Sadie won't talk to her mother without blowing up. And Cheryl is very critical and unforgiving of Sadie."

Bert's role of peacemaker originally came from his need to protect his tiny daughter Sadie from Cheryl's critical attitude. Though Sadie is twenty-three, Bert still feels the need to intervene to keep peace in the family. Both women rely on his intervention, even conducting most of their communication indirectly through Bert. Each complains to him about the other because they are unable to resolve anything between themselves.

Bert continued, "I sometimes feel like I have two daughters that I have to keep from fighting. Cheryl isn't any better at resolving things than Sadie. It's been this way since Sadie was a child."

As Bert is describing here, the buffering partner frequently views himself as the more mature or parental one who needs to keep the peace by acting as the go-between. It is the common result of a child being enmeshed with one parent and disengaged from the other. The buffering partner, however, is unwittingly contributing to the problem and must reexamine the protectionism. Though I have used the example of a dad buffering a mother and a child, the usual pattern is the opposite. Most go-between communication or buffering is done by the mother between Dad and the kids.

Go-Between Moms

Probably the most common pattern of buffering in our culture has Mom as the go-between with the kids and Dad. Dad becomes the go-between when the mother is disengaged from the child, but when Mom bonds with one or more of the kids and Dad doesn't, Mom becomes the buffer. This puts the pressure on Mom to do all the parenting and communicating with the kids. Dad is passive, absent, or angry. He is unable or unwilling to become jointly involved in parenting any or all of the children. Because Dad is absent, remote, or threatening, the kids go to Mom for everything.

My family was a lot like that. Dad worked long hours and had an explosive temper. Mom was sensitive and caring, more than willing to meet our needs and make up for Dad's deficiencies. We always went to Mom when we needed something, and she would talk to Dad about it. Susan's family worked much the same way. Her dad was unavailable because he was too involved with his work. When he was home, he was pleasant but emotionally distant. She and her siblings also went to their mom for everything.

Our moms became the go-betweens who tried to fill the gap left by our dads' lack of parenting and emotional involvement. They fulfilled their own roles and took on the responsibility of helping their husbands fulfill their roles. When one parent does not spend needed time with the kids—like Susan's father—or when one parent has a problem with anger—like my father—the other parent may take on more responsibility to protect the children.

However, the parent acting as a go-between may take on more responsibility than is healthy or required. The go-between parent feels pressured to remedy the situation. This may provoke the parent to go to excessive lengths to protect the child and make up for the deficient parent. A common result of go-between patterns is manipulation and dishonesty. Though the go-between parent may have good intentions, the parent's attempt at change is wrong, and unhealthy patterns result.

Rebekah's Manipulation

Once again the Bible offers us an example of an unhealthy family dynamic through the life of a prominent woman named Rebekah and her son Jacob. The wife of a wealthy man, Rebekah favored her son Jacob over his twin Esau. When their father, Isaac, was advanced in years and blind, he wanted to pass on his blessing to Esau, the older twin, whom he favored. Knowing that, Rebekah schemed against her husband's plan. She told Jacob to go into Isaac's tent dressed as Esau and receive the blessing. Jacob did as he was told, deceiving his father and stealing the blessing from his brother. Rebekah's protection of Jacob prompted her to manipulate and deceive her husband. She wanted the blessing for her favored son.

Though many people who act as go-betweens manipulate their spouses to help their children, the ends do not justify the means. Jacob had to flee his brother's wrath, and he also became known as a schemer, like his mother. Jacob reaped what he sowed when his father-in-law schemed against him and did not give him the woman he wanted for a wife. The lesson learned by the protected child may be one of manipulation and deceit, and the manipulated result may not be a desirable one.

Protecting Too Much

"What am I supposed to do when he won't talk to the kids?" my client asked. "All he does is bark orders at them, getting angry if they don't immediately do what he tells them to. Am I supposed to let him abuse them?"

Her response is the normal one for a go-between mother when she is challenged with the notion that she is providing too much buffering between the kids and their angry dad. She is concerned about her children's well-being and therefore feels it is her obligation to protect them. Many go-between patterns like hers are designed to keep the kids from suffering the harshness or abuse of the other parent. They do not evolve only from disengagement. Regardless of origin, protectionism must be carefully examined and made appropriate for the child's age and family situation. Reshaping healthy bonds of love requires that the overly protectionistic bond be lessened. The re-created family is one of balanced love, protection, and individual responsibility.

I am not implying that it is always wrong to protect a child from an angry parent. A small child certainly needs protection from a hurtful parent. It is every father's or mother's responsibility to protect a child from abuse; and in cases of physical or sexual abuse, a safe place outside the home may be necessary. In fact, when conflict in the family has reached the crisis point of physical abuse, it is almost always necessary to get outside help to resolve the problems. Crisis centers and free counseling are available in almost every city. If you or someone in your family is being physically or sexually abused, it is absolutely essential for you to get help from a competent professional.

In many families, the abuse is not physical but emotional. In these difficult situations it is wise, as the child grows, to reexamine the need for being the go-between. When the appropriate protection of a young child is continued throughout adolescence, the result can be hurtful. By late adolescence a child needs to be able to relate in a healthy way to a hurtful or angry parent. We have been talking about a child growing up into something; the something needs to be a healthy individual who can develop and enforce appropriate boundaries, responding rather than reacting to the poorly functioning parent.

Healthy family members create strong, healthy families. The adolescent needs support and instruction in dealing with the difficult parent in a healthy manner rather than being protected from the parent. This is much like the task of the Peace Corps; we send volunteers to Third World countries to teach the people how to improve their lot rather than do it all for them.

However, even in the instruction in how to respond to the problematic parent, care must be taken. Managing the relationship with a hurtful parent requires the adolescent to work with personal feelings and honestly confront the parent's behavior. An adolescent who does not learn how to do this before leaving home will be hampered in future relationships, not knowing how to resolve hurt, anger, or fear and honestly deal with hurtful people. The adolescent will tiptoe around others or expect Mom and, by extension, others to soothe the hurts and offer protection from life.

In my family, Mom was the go-between for us with Dad and his rage. She intervened on our behalf, always soothing our wounds and making excuses for his abusive behavior. Her protectionism extended into adult life, even though she and Dad separated over his anger. As a result, it took longer for me and, I think, some of my brothers to resolve our feelings toward Dad and create a relationship with him without Mom's advice or help. We had been too dependent on her.

The enmeshed parent usually makes the mistake of protecting children too long and further compounds the problem by failing to teach them how to respond to the other parent in a healthy manner. When a mother does too good a job of making up for an absent, angry, or neglectful father, she becomes both father and mother to her kids. The pattern carries into children's adulthood when Mom will always say "we" or "your dad and I" instead of letting Dad speak for himself or saying what she alone thinks.

In another variation of this situation the mother will speak for herself but will caution the kids about what or what not to say to Dad, encouraging them to develop patterns of secrecy and manipulation. She becomes the all-wise buffer who is always trying to fix the relationship with Dad by working on it behind the scenes. Children easily learn this style of resolving problems and become manipulative and circuitous when confronted with difficult relationship issues.

I feared honest and open confrontation with Dad and others. I never had to push past my anger and fear and confront my dad over his abusive behavior. Mom always did it for me. In adult years I had to learn how to confront others in appropriate ways. The overprotectionism, though necessary when I was young, stifled my growth in later years because it continued too long.

Communication patterns that always revolve around Mom keep the kids from knowing firsthand what Dad really thinks and feels. Communication becomes distorted when passed through another. Have you ever played the game of gossip? You whisper a secret into someone's ear; that person passes it to the next person, who in turn whispers it to the next. When the secret is finally whispered back into your ear, the message has changed in emphasis or content. This is what happens in families where one parent tries to play the game of go-between. The shielding parent's agenda gets mixed in with the communication to the children, either softening the message or distorting it to serve what the parent thinks is best for the children. In the long run, this scenario creates more barriers to closeness, keeping the children from directly facing their dad and working out their issues.

Susan's mother and mine never realized how being the go-between for so long resulted in increasing the distance between us and our dads instead of closing the gap. We got used to a distant relationship with our fathers. When we were older, establishing the closeness we desired in childhood was difficult.

When one parent tries too hard to make up for the failure of the other, the results are rarely good. The problem with disengagement between a parent and a child is that it will directly affect the child, and it will provoke the other parent to buffer, overdo, and overprotect. Part of the answer to re-creating a healthy family environment of love when one parent is disengaged is to make sure the other parent does not mishandle the reaction to the problem, thus worsening an already unsettled situation. Closeness and protection are valuable but not in excess and not during every developmental cycle of the child's growth into adulthood.

Disengaged Moms and Dads

The last disengagement scenario is one in which both parents are distant. When the original bonding with parents goes awry, the child tends to remake the family system, finding new "parents" to be close to. The child who bonds to neither Mom nor Dad may bond to another family member or close friend. Bonding to a brother or sister is common, as is growing close to a cousin, neighborhood friend, grandparent, aunt, or uncle. Each relationship becomes a substitute for the lack of parental closeness. Though helpful during certain times of life, these surrogate parental bonds also have their downside.

Susan did not bond closely to her mother, but she was very close to her younger sister who became her substitute mom, always nurturing, loving, and accepting. They preserved a close relationship even into adulthood. The relationship was so close that it became an issue in the early years of our marriage. Susan trusted her sister more than me, and she shared her heart with her sister rather than with me. When we fought, which in those days was frequent, she sought solace from her sister and relied on her to be a go-between in resolving our fights.

Initially helpful, the pattern later prevented us from learning how to face and resolve our problems. It also encouraged Susan's disengagement from me and dependence on her sister. Susan did not easily risk the vulnerability and intimacy our marriage required. She sought intimacy and connectedness with her sister, who was safe, nurturing, and permissive. The connection between them put me in competition with her sister for Susan's time, attention, and favor.

A husband or wife who is very closely bonded to another

family member will have difficulty entering into the intimacy and closeness the marriage covenant demands. The close tie with the other must be forsaken before intimacy can develop between the marriage partners. In our situation, Susan had to withdraw from the supportive protection and intimacy of her sister to bond to me.

Although initially soothing, substitute alliances can be harmful. A younger sister is not a healthy substitute for a mature parent. Additionally, the substitute parent's motivation for caring can be born out of *that person's* needs for a close relationship with someone. The coming together of two needy people may seem to be a healthy match, but the relationship is vulnerable to unhealthy patterns. An older sister may take care of a younger sister, but when the younger one needs her freedom, the older sister may resist. Her need to parent her sister requires that the younger sister remain loyal and appreciative of her efforts.

Many older sibling–younger sibling bonds formed in childhood sour in adulthood. In my wife's case her oldest sister, like many firstborns, was a surrogate parent to all the younger brothers and sisters. In adulthood each of the brothers and sisters resisted her attempt at continued parenting and control, causing conflict and hurt feelings. Once a sibling adopts a surrogate or substitute role with another sibling, it is very hard to let go of the role and become just a caring and supportive brother or sister. Substitute parental bonds are not free from difficulty, and they do not provide the trust, safety, and protection from a responsible adult that children require.

The Disengagement Checklist

"Do you have a set of characteristics I can read or a series of questions that would help me know if I am or have been disengaged from my family?" questioned a client.

Disengaged individuals may not realize that they tend to be disengaged in relationships or that they were disengaged from the family while growing up. The following characteristics are typical of individuals who come from disengaged backgrounds or need more connection in their present families:

• The individuals don't know how to be emotionally intimate with others or may feel uncomfortable or fearful of being too close.

• They don't share their inner feelings easily or often. They prefer not to let others know how they truly feel and may not even know their feelings, other than irritation or anger.

• Physical displays of affection and verbal "I care" messages are infrequent or offered only when another initiates. There may even be an awkwardness with showing or receiving direct "I care" messages.

• Disengaged individuals resist being vulnerable. They will rarely ask for help or share their needs with others.

• When bothered or offended by another person, disengaged individuals will normally respond by withdrawal and the cold shoulder. If not withdrawing, they will strike out angrily or critically.

- Oftentimes disengaged persons are loners who prefer to reenergize by being alone, doing their own thing rather than connecting or socializing with others.

- Disengaged individuals may complain about feeling claustrophobic in a relationship. They like the mystique of the "rugged individualist" and consciously or unconsciously embrace such themes as "I want my space"; "I don't need anyone"; "I can take care of it myself."

As the list indicates, individuals who tend toward disengagement have a limited ability or desire for intimate relationship. Obviously, re-creating family means challenging the disengagement and creating the connections of love that are lacking or were lost.

Love Hunger and Codependency

Perhaps the greatest problem with parental disengagement is that it creates a wound and a love hunger in the child that are not easily resolved even though substitutes may exist. In the movie *On Golden Pond,* Jane Fonda plays the part of a grown woman who, after a failed marriage, is still seeking the approval and love from her father that she never got as a child. This theme of seeking the love never provided in childhood is common to many of us. The lack of intimate love and resultant love hunger for parents produce a deep need in the child to be loved, cared for, and appreciated. The child misses the affirmation that only intimate connectedness with the mother and father was meant to bring. As the movie showcased, even in adulthood the child within may still unsuccessfully vie for Mom's or Dad's approval and attention. One way this is done is through trying to please Mom or Dad even at great personal cost. Daughters and sons seeking the absent or disengaged father's approval is a familiar scenario.

The pattern is also frequently seen in daughter-mother relationships. Though a successful marketing executive, Ann Devaney was still trying to get her mom's approval. "I'm a mature forty-year-old woman, and I'm still afraid of my mother's disapproval," Ann said. "It's discouraging! You would think that all of this would clear up after you grow up. But every time I'm around her I find myself saying and doing things to keep her from being angry with me and to get her to like me."

Ann's frustration is common to many adults who are still trying to overcome childhood barriers and create closeness with their parents. The disengagement of childhood pressures the adult child to love, care, or give the parent whatever is necessary to gain the connection the childhood lacked. I did that with my dad. Because he and I were not close, I performed to make him proud of me. I wanted the closeness, approval, and connection that I lacked in earlier years. My response to our disengagement was to adopt a codependent style of loving in which I went the extra mile to remain connected and loved, and he still remained distant, never calling or visiting me.

I was wounded by the lack of mutual love and connection with my dad, and I knew it. I could feel the hurt, and tears came easily when I thought of our relationship. Mourning my childhood lack and relinquishing the dream that I would ever have the closeness and love I craved were my steps to freedom. I forgave Dad's deficiencies and committed myself to having a healthy relationship in which I would honor and respect him without expecting anything in return. Giving up the dream was the hardest part. It took time, tears, and a lot of prayer. My lack of parental love was a deep wound in my spirit, and I needed God to heal me.

Counterdependent Love Hunger

Many people from disengaged backgrounds respond to their wounds by developing counterdependent styles of getting and giving love. As children, they do not learn the value or skills of closeness. As adults, they fear the vulnerability and engulfment that dependency on others can create. Even though they have a deep inner love hunger, they are not willing to go to any lengths, as codependent people do, to fulfill it. Their lack of bonding from the past makes intimacy and connectedness a risky venture. Counterdependent people are used to being alone and are not comfortable with the transparency and risk of intimate relationship. They lack the trust element of relationship that comes from intimate childhood bonding. Counterdependent people require others to initiate bonding, and it is difficult for them to initiate and maintain healthy relationships. In great part they expect others to love, care, and give to them in ways they never experienced from their parents. Even when others do so, they tend to push them away, feeling uncomfortable with the intimacy and pressure for relationship.

Susan's lack of bonding with both parents encouraged her counterdependent style of relating. Her unspoken motto in our marriage was "my way or the highway," while mine was "your way controls my way." She needed to resolve the disengaged bonding patterns of her past. Resolve came when the crisis of our marital problems forced her to face the hidden pain. Counterdependent people must scratch below the surface of their feelings, peel back the scar tissue, and look for the wounds. Usually, the pain of a crisis prompts them to become willing to examine their wounds.

Change came when Susan recanted her vow not to feel the pain or be vulnerable. Once the wound was opened, she also mourned her loss and worked toward releasing the dream of being perfectly loved, approved of, or cared for by her parents or others. Forgiveness also came—but slowly. Various life events prompted Susan to probe further into her childhood patterns and brought deeper and deeper release. Again, parental wounds take time, effort, and God's help to heal.

The Danger of Abuse

The re-created family provides a safe and trusting environment for its children. The connections of love not only nurture but also protect in healthy ways. As we have seen, disengagement from parents is very common and creates emotional wounds. In a small percentage of families it can have another serious side effect. It makes the children vulnerable to abuse by others. Sexual abusers of young children often deceive or entice them initially by offering the closeness, attention, and love they so desperately need but are not getting from their parents.

A young client shared the following observation about her sexual abuse during one of our sessions: "I couldn't tell Mom what happened with Uncle Ray because I thought it was my fault, that I had done something wrong. I didn't want her to get angry with me. We never got along very well, and she was always on my back about something. I just couldn't say anything to her, and there was no one else I could tell."

The child's lack of close bonding with her mom prevented

her from fully divulging what happened. She was not close to her mother, and her dad was rarely home. Her mom was also angry and critical of her much of the time. The atmosphere of trust and acceptance that would have allowed her to share how Uncle Ray molested her was absent. Parents of an abused child often wonder why the child never told them what happened, not understanding that the abuser may have threatened the child with harm, blamed the abuse on the child, or even threatened to harm the parents.

No matter how threatening the abuser is, a closely bonded child will be more inclined to risk telling parents the truth if the child knows on a heart level that he or she can trust fears, shame, and heart to Mom and Dad. Most children will not divulge abuse unless close bonding is present, the trust and heartfelt closeness that emotional connection brings.

Creating New Bonds of Love

For many people, the work of re-creating family must focus on overcoming disengagement and creating new ways of sharing love. Disengaged individuals can change the way they relate. They can also learn how to bond with others in healthy ways. Susan shed the painful legacy of her past and committed herself to learning how to intimately connect. Facing her fears and taking baby steps toward change worked. Sharing activities, sharing feelings, and practicing direct "I care" messages were Susan's how-tos of change. But perhaps the most important aspect of change for the counterdependent person is making the decision to push past discomfort and experiment with closeness and intimacy.

I remember an instance when Susan committed to doing a direct "I care" message at least once a day for an entire month. "It was hard and I didn't want to do it," she said. "But it didn't kill me, and as a matter of fact, I got to where I actually enjoyed it. It also helped me enlarge my comfort zone."

Once counterdependent people become comfortable with the enriching feelings of intimacy, they increase their motivation to change. Like any pattern, a new pattern of love takes time, commitment, and assistance to establish. Though at first it may not come naturally, over time the feelings will change.

Family bonding patterns are the activating influences of future relationship. If as children we are not appropriately close to both parents, problems in intimacy result. The disengagement patterns of the family of origin create love hungers within us that will show themselves in our deficient patterns of getting and giving love. The codependent or counterdependent love pattern is acted out and reinforced over and over again in our relationships with people we love. We unconsciously act out the family legacy by trying to re-create a new one that will give us the love or closeness we lacked and therefore desperately need. In doing this we blindly set ourselves up for failure rather than success because we are unaware of the forces that motivate much of our behavior. Recreating family requires that we recognize the hurtful legacies, release the power they have over our lives, and adopt new ways of loving.

The more we look at family life, the clearer it becomes that there are no perfect parents in this world. We have all suffered from the mistakes of our parents, and we continue to make mistakes that harm our children. Despite this, Susan and I have discovered that there is one perfect Parent. In relationship with God, we have found a Father who understands and loves us perfectly, even when we don't deserve it. Through

His grace, many of the wounds of childhood have been healed. Through His mercy, our faults and shortcomings have been forgiven. Through His wisdom, we are learning together how to love each other and our children.

If you are discovering and feeling hurt from your legacy of disengagement, try the following prayer. Many people have found healing through sharing their pain in prayer with a God who cares. As you face and resolve your pain, remember that actions, prayers, and God's grace go hand in hand.

Dear heavenly Father,

I recognize that my _____ *(mother, father, or both)* was *(were)* not there for me. For whatever reason _____ *(he, she, or they)* was *(were)* unable to bless me by lovingly bonding to me. _____ *(Mom, Dad, or They)* did not make me feel valuable by drawing me intimately close. As a result I have suffered feelings of _____ *(loneliness, loss, deadness, hurt, self-hatred, etc.)* and have also lived out unhealthy bonding patterns with my own _____ *(children, husband, wife, relationships, etc.).*

Please, Father, help me to release the pain of my past and re-create enduring patterns of healthy love for the future. Be the close and caring parent to me that I have never had. Heal my heart and change me. Amen.

In the following section we will explore how legacies of closeness and disengagement are acted out in the marriage relationship. We will also observe how romance and attraction are closely tied to the family post and how healthy marital intimacy can be fashioned.

PART 3

MAKING MARRIAGE WORK

A family is created by a marriage. As the marriage goes, so does the family. It is the task of a new marriage to bring together two separate histories, values, and sets of needs, and forge a new combined whole, one that becomes a healthy legacy for all its members.

CHAPTER 5

Come Close
. . . Stay Away

How should two loving hearts compose and
mingle into one?

—Thomas Kibble Hervey

Marriage is the foundational relationship of family life. All other relationships take shape from the marriage; that is, family life and its relationship patterns are shaped and controlled by Mom and Dad and their relationship. If the marriage is healthy, the other relationships can be healthy. If the marriage is not working, the rest of the family will register the impact. It's as though the marriage is the thermostat with the family members registering the temperature. Perhaps the most influential marital issue in need of resolve is that of emotional closeness. How well spouses resolve the need for being close or distant influences the stability of the marriage and the love patterns of the rest of the family.

This struggle over intimacy and closeness is at the very heart of most marriage problems. It's the push-pull that keeps the marriage from stability and fulfillment. It is an imbalance found in the relationship of many married couples. One partner wants more closeness while the other seems to want less. Frequently, the wife desires intimacy, complaining that her husband is more interested in watching football than in talking to her. Although some view this as a natural difference between the sexes, it should more correctly be understood as the result of childhood bonding patterns. In my marriage, I have been the one who has more often desired closeness. When I pushed for intimacy, Susan felt stifled and needed distance. We argued, blamed, and fought over who was right and who was wrong.

She said, "You're smothering me. Just give me some space!"

I countered, "You're more interested in that book than in me!"

This struggle over closeness is also at the very root of romantic attraction. The selection of a spouse is deeply influenced by the emotional bonding of childhood, though most people are totally unaware of its power. We believe that falling in love is a rather mysterious and inexplicable process when in fact, it can often be easily understood by looking at the bonding patterns of the past. In this and the following chapters, we will explore the dynamics of marital closeness and attraction. Both are shaped by the love patterns of the family past.

Family Legacies

My parents' marital struggle over intimacy resulted in unhealthy relationship patterns within our family. Unable to satisfactorily meet each other's needs, Mom turned to the kids for emotional closeness, and Dad worked harder. When I was a child, my mom confided in me her pain and disappointment in her relationship with Dad. In feeling sorry for her, I made it my responsibility to comfort her and try to make her feel better. I took on the burden of her feelings and made it my obligation to care for her emotional health. The role I played with my mother extended into my relationships with all women. I needed to be needed. I became a magnet, drawing to myself women who were in need, especially in need of me and my kind of love. People who learn to take care of others will often attract and be selectively attracted to very needy partners. This is both a strength and a weakness.

The strength is in the caretakers' ability to enter into intimacy so easily. The weakness is that their need for closeness causes them to do all the work of the marriage for all the wrong reasons. They attempt to re-create the close feelings of intimacy they had in childhood while at the same time blaming their partners for being too distant. They focus on their partners' inabilities rather than their own hidden motivations.

I watched Susan all the time to see if she was upset with, happy with, or interested in me. When she was moody, I tiptoed around her to make sure she wasn't offended with me. I went to extremes to try to keep her happy, pleasing and caring for her, trying to avoid rejection and recapture the feelings of intimate connectedness that I had come to associate with love. I was living out a codependent pattern of relationship.

Spouses of enmeshed people develop another set of problems. They both appreciate and despise the lavish love they receive. Though they may value it at times, they can also feel violated, pressured, and pushed into intimacy. Enmeshed people tend to be too invasive in their drive to be intimate, push-ing their partners to become detached and autonomous in response.

As we have seen, people from disengaged backgrounds are emotionally distant. They tend to value autonomy and need a lot of time and space for themselves, becoming counter-dependent in their relationships. They may have had hurts in childhood that caused them to use distance to protect them-selves, or they may have had parents who were distant and never taught them how to be close to others. Inwardly, they may have a strong need for closeness and love, but at the same time they fear intimacy and hold others at arm's length. This was Susan's legacy. Her ambivalence made her seek partners who appeared safe to love and who would not reject her. Because I would go the extra mile, giving and caring exces-sively, it offered her the combination of love and safety she needed. This made for a powerful dynamic of attraction be-tween us.

Susan once described how she was first attracted to me: "A group of us were driving to Flagstaff when we had a flat tire. Al immediately took charge, fixed the flat, and got us on our way. I remember thinking what a good father he would be. I didn't realize at the time that what I was really feeling was what a good father he would be to *me!*"

My caretaking qualities were attractive to Susan. As with other women from disengaged backgrounds, Susan wanted someone she could trust to take care of her. She wanted a guarantee that she would feel secure, safe, and loved. She wanted a spouse to be both a lover and a caring, involved parent she never had. Susan needed me to prove my love by providing her with abundant attention and affirmation, and she self-protectively withdrew if I disappointed her; yet at the same time she mistrusted intimacy and was unable to let me get too close. A come close–stay away dynamic was created; she desired deep intimacy and closeness and then in the next breath wanted distance and separation. Hence the mixed messages of come close–stay away.

Susan found it difficult to maintain the intimacy that marriage requires. On the other hand, I found it difficult not to have constant intimacy. She was reliving her family legacy of having been too distant for too long, and I was reliving mine of being too close for too long.

For years neither of us realized that we both needed change. The battle raged until we both began to understand our differing needs for closeness and independence and how our childhood experiences had shaped us. I particularly remember a conversation when I finally admitted to Susan that the problem of closeness wasn't just hers. This realization was important. Codependent people or individuals from enmeshed backgrounds, like me, think that we can never be too close. We strongly believe in the value of shared hearts and intimate feelings. When others don't meet our expectations, we blame them instead of understanding that our need may be too great and our belief too strong.

"Honey, I can't tell you how much this means to me," Susan responded. "Even though I have argued with you and resisted your comments about my disengagement, deep down inside I felt it was also my fault. Your willingness to admit you have a part in our problem helps me lower defenses and admit my contribution."

The push-pull struggle is a reflection of both people's past and current needs. Both need to admit their contribution. I was reluctant to do so not only because of my beliefs about closeness but also because I was afraid Susan would think that she didn't have a problem, that it was all my fault. This fear keeps many partners from being honest about their contribution to the marital problem. However, change comes only when truth surfaces and blame stops.

After my admission to Susan, both of us were able to agree to our contribution and commit to work toward change together. Taking steps into the past for healing helped each of us resolve the empowering roots. We also agreed to a plan for dealing with the issue in the future. Instead of criticizing Susan by saying, "You've been too distant lately," I would say, "Honey, I'm feeling the need for more attention and affection. Could you help me out?" Susan stopped accusing me of being smothering and instead requested time out for herself. The positive, nonaccusatory interactions minimized our hurt feelings and anger while allowing for behaviors that helped us meet our needs.

Exceptions to the Rules

Though most enmeshed people are givers and most disengaged people are takers, other relationship patterns can develop and should be examined. Enmeshed children can bond to their parents in such a way that creates severe dependency in adulthood. When children are catered to and emotionally indulged throughout childhood, they learn how to be takers instead of givers. They expect others to initiate and maintain relationships because that is their learned style. Overprotected and spoiled, they require others to take responsibility for their happiness, expecting them to "fix" any negative feelings they experience. They are most aptly described as emotionally spoiled individuals. As a result, they become self-centered and unable to fully participate in the give-and-take of a healthy relationship. They become like disengaged people, attracted to partners who will give, care, and love too much.

Do you remember the movie *Gone with the Wind* starring Vivian Leigh as the beautiful, yet immature, Scarlett O'Hara? Scarlett was spoiled and emotionally pampered by her father and nanny.. Though she loved Rhett Butler, she was unable to shed her legacy of self-centeredness and forge a healthy response to him. Eventually, he gave up and left her. Scarlett's inability to love was a result of mismanaged parenting.

Though most individuals from disengaged backgrounds remain emotionally distant throughout life, the powerful love hunger of some disengaged individuals propels them into going the extra mile in relationships. They become the givers in one-way relationships, loving and caring too much to get the love they never had.

Whether one comes from a disengaged or an enmeshed background, recognizing the resultant deficient codependent and counterdependent love patterns is the beginning of change. As Susan and I have faced the past and committed to improving the present, we have been able to forge more healthy and fulfilling love patterns. Our push-pull struggle has lessened a great deal with time and effort.

Bonding and Sexuality

Sexual intimacy and expression are also affected by the family past. For example, in women the love hunger created by a disengaged background frequently translates into seductive behaviors or sexual actions aimed at getting the approval and attention they needed in childhood. This behavior is especially prevalent if the emotional distance or rejection was between girls and their fathers. The young women will telegraph sexuality yet rarely enjoy the resulting sex. They are prone to give sex to get love—all in a vain attempt to have men fill the void of the childhood years. Such young women can present a highly desirable image of sexual appeal, flavored with an air of vulnerability, inviting men to give them the attention they want to receive sexual gratification.

This style of relating, however, is rarely emotionally or sexually fulfilling for either partner. It frequently encourages promiscuity and results in inhibited sexual desire in marriage because this kind of woman does not really enjoy sex as much as attention. She uses sex as a means of gaining attention, affection, or security. Once she is married, the sexual bargaining chip stops working, so sexual intimacy goes out the window.

Men from disengaged backgrounds often take a different path. They give love to get sex. Their lack of parental bonding encouraged them to develop patterns of self-comfort and closeness primarily through sexual means. Unable to maintain and enjoy emotional intimacy in long-term relationships, they resort to sexual expression to make connection with others. Their compulsive sexual desire will provoke them to give women all the attention they desire to get the sex they crave. Once they are married, their wives will frequently complain about their behavior.

A client, June, protested to me, "The only time he ever pays attention to me is when he wants sex. He is never affectionate unless he's touching my breasts or some other part of me. I think the only reason he makes up after a fight or says he's sorry is because he's missing the sex!"

A man from a disengaged background who is also invested in sex will have difficulty handling the intimacy that marriage requires. The push-pull struggle will center on the bedroom, with the wife demanding more love and attention and the husband more sex and less complaining. Until the root issues from the past are faced and resolved, both will find only marginal fulfillment in their marriage. The sexual struggle must be resolved through taking many of the same steps that Susan and I took to resolve our battle over closeness. Both dynamics are the result of past love patterns that are inhibiting current fulfillment. When partners recognize the pattern and work on resolving the past and making new plans for the future, they can begin to change. In *Released to Love: Healing the Barriers That Hinder Sexual Intimacy and Fulfillment,* I detail how bonding patterns and other influences create these and other kinds of sexual problems and how God brings healing.

The Prison of Patterns

Did you ever watch the television comedy "All in the Family"? Archie and Edith Bunker and their daughter Gloria and her husband, Mike, presented a wry weekly commentary on family life. Archie and Edith displayed a classic one-way marriage, with Archie as the taker and Edith as the giver. Archie continually criticized Edith and the rest of the family. He figured that as long as he put bread and butter on the table, he didn't have to do much of anything else. Edith waited on him hand and foot. She thought it was her role to clean the house, cook the meals, and take care of everyone. Sensitive and caring, Edith was constantly trying to tone down Archie's insensitive commentary and to manipulate things behind the scenes to keep Archie happy. "Oh, Gloria, don't let your dad find that out or he'll get maaaaaad!" was a frequent admonition.

I vividly remember an episode in which Edith got a job.

For a week, she came home too late and too tired to get dinner for Archie. When his blustery demands were ignored, he finally changed them to gentle entreaties, hoping that Edith would once again cater to his needs. Archie never seemed to prize close caring or a sensitive relationship. His bottom line message was, "It's my way or the highway. If you're unhappy, why don't you leave?" He prized his independence and feared being vulnerable; yet when Edith quit being his caretaker, he went into a tailspin. It took a crisis of life like Edith's newfound work role to make him willing to risk expressing his need for her. The value of crisis in a marriage should never be underestimated. It can be a time of growth and change or of dissolution and worsened patterns. It depends on the responses of the partners.

My dad was much like Archie Bunker. He prized his independence because of his painful past. He had to raise himself and felt he couldn't rely on anyone. His emotional wounds caused him to fear vulnerability and dependence. When he and Mom reached a crisis in their marriage, he found it very difficult to change. He was devastated when she left him but still unable to admit that he needed to do something about it. He could not risk what was needed to make the relationship work.

He spent hours tearfully mourning her departure but could never simply say, "I'm sorry. Please forgive me. I'll change." The disengagement of his past created a lonely private world of despair that prevented change and vulnerability. He wanted closeness but feared it. The hurtful emotional strongholds of his past controlled him, preventing him from giving and getting the love he so desperately needed.

A client, Henry Vasquez, experienced a marital crisis very similar to my dad's. Henry was a career miner who had risen to the position of level boss in one of Arizona's copper mines. After years of working hard and raising a family, his wife left him because he refused to deal with his disengagement and bad temper. Henry's wife, Gloria, begged him numerous times to go to counseling. Raised in the "macho" environment of a mining town, Henry thought counseling was only needed if someone was "sick in the head." He also boasted that he "didn't need anyone telling him what to do." However, when Gloria left, his world caved in. The kids told him that he shouldn't be so proud and that if he wanted her back, he ought to go to counseling.

When Gloria refused to return, Henry agreed to the counseling. Gloria welcomed the change of heart and readily participated as well. Henry didn't let the crisis reinforce his bitterness and resistance; he recognized it as an opportunity for change. When the pressure for change is evident, a willingness to face the challenge and create new and healthier patterns of love will always pay off.

Journey to Re-Creation

Disengaged individuals want closeness—but only on their terms. Enmeshed individuals want too much closeness and will pursue it on anyone's terms. Though they are attracted to each other like powerful magnets, their relationship becomes a drama of push and pull. When the enmeshed person pushes hard for relationship, the disengaged one pulls away. When the enmeshed partner pulls back, the disengaged one will step slightly past the comfort zone and invite pursuit again. There develops an intricate dance of dependence and independence, intimacy and detachment, love and withdrawal. Most relationships include such a dance because most of us come from backgrounds with some degree of enmeshment and disengagement.

Come close–stay away relationship patterns require balancing to produce healthy love. In the unique combining of traits and the meeting of individual needs the marriage, and therefore the family, flourishes and finds its balance. When marriage partners face their love hungers and patterns of the past and begin to mutually care for each other's needs, the marriage stabilizes.

Henry and Gloria Vasquez began their journey to change and re-creation together. They were willing to do the painful work of restructuring their patterns of communication and the ways they shared love and intimacy. In follow-up counseling sessions, both have admitted to me they have lapses and still fight. But they are working their fights through to resolution rather than letting issues simmer beneath the surface waiting to explode.

"Our life together isn't totally peaceful," Henry observed with a grin, "but I think our level of commitment is greater than it's ever been."

In the next chapter, we will further examine the ways in which family love patterns influence the selection of a life partner and the structure of marriage.

CHAPTER 6

The Paradox of Romantic Attraction

Where does the family start? It starts with a young man falling in love with a girl. No superior alternative has yet been found.

—Winston Churchill

The love patterns of the family past play an often hidden, yet controlling, role in the drama of romantic attraction. Who we are attracted to and what we do about it set the stage for the love patterns of marriage. The family is created by marriage. As the marriage goes, so does the family. How partners resolve the need to get and give love will establish the family's patterns of closeness and distance, disengagement or enmeshment, the ones that produce the love patterns of the next generation. Understanding and resolving the paradox of romantic attraction can assist a couple in re-creating healthy patterns of love that enrich the marriage and endure the generations. That was the challenge for Bob and Janelle Gatewood. Recently married, they were experiencing problems.

Athletic and handsome, Bob came from a family of southern gentlemen who were raised by nannies. Janelle, a blonde fitness buff from California, was vivacious and self-assured. When Janelle met Bob, she instantly fell in love with his soft-spoken manner and childlike behavior.

Bob shared how they first met: "I never knew what it was like to be close to anyone until I met Janelle. I was playing on the fraternity baseball team and twisted my ankle sliding into second base. Reacting quickly, Janelle packed it in ice, and as she fussed over me, she talked freely, asking me all kinds of personal questions. I thought to myself, *Wow!*"

Bob's attraction was based on Janelle's disarming, intimate manner. She was exciting, caring, and sensitive, all at the same time. She both unsettled and intrigued him. Janelle could tell she made an impression on him. She felt the challenge of finding out who the quiet man was. Somehow his reserve encouraged her pursuit. After a whirlwind courtship, they married that same year before school was out; however, problems began shortly afterward.

Janelle said, "I would wait up wanting to talk and share, but he only wanted to watch TV or have sex. I spent many a night hurt and angry, begging him to talk to me. But the answer was always the same, 'Why are you pushing me so much? Can't you tell I'm tired?' I guess I finally got tired of asking for his company. He was acting just like my dad, never talking and always going off to do something by himself."

From this vignette, we can see the Gatewoods were living out the results of their family bonding legacies. Neither one was aware that past patterns of closeness had played a key role in attracting them to each other as well as helping to create their current problems. Growing up, Janelle had been too close to her mother, who was disabled. Her life had centered on caring for her mom's physical and emotional needs. Janelle was also starved for her father's attention. He was rarely available to her, working hour after hour in the garage in his spare time instead of spending it with his family. Being a caretaker came naturally to her, as did her attraction to Bob, a man who shared many of her father's good qualities. Initially, he showed promise of meeting her deep need for love.

Bob Gatewood had never known what it was like to be close to anyone. His mother and father never bonded with him emotionally, leaving the task of raising him to various nannies who had preferred a younger, more outgoing brother over him.

Bob said, "My nannies took good care of me. I never wanted for anything. They fed me, clothed me, and did everything for me. It never occurred to me to share my inner thoughts or feelings with them. I kept things pretty much to myself. It was uncomfortable for me to have Janelle ask me how I felt about something. A part of me didn't know what I felt, and another part didn't want to talk about it even if I did."

Bob's legacy of disengagement resulted in his need to be taken care of emotionally. He wanted someone to love him, but he didn't know how to return the feeling. He was ill-equipped for the relational demands that marriage and closeness require. Janelle's natural caretaking initially filled his need to be nurtured; but soon the marriage was experiencing difficulty because Janelle felt unloved and Bob felt pressured and criticized. Their love was turning to hate. They needed to resolve the contradiction inherent in all romantic attractions.

The Paradox of Attraction

Each of us carries into adulthood a cherished dream of being loved perfectly. Parents never love us perfectly because they are imperfect. Their lack creates within us a powerful and often unconscious need to seek out and find the love we never fully received.

Janelle ardently yearned for a man to pay attention to her. Her father had been pleasant, even charming, but always remote and unavailable. Bob needed the attention and affection he missed in childhood. They were a perfect match for each other. Janelle would initiate the love Bob needed while he would respond with the attention Janelle desired. Difficulties developed when Janelle wanted more of his attention than he felt comfortable giving. Bob wanted her care and concern but not when they were accompanied with too much pressure on him to reciprocate. Ironically, the very qualities that attracted them to each other were the seeds of their later problems.

Bob and Janelle Gatewood had conflicting needs, but perhaps more problematic was their conflict of styles. With Janelle's caretaking qualities came inherent behaviors of pushing for interaction, heartfelt sharing, and total transparency. For a disengaged individual like Bob, such behavior soon felt suffocating. He was ill equipped for the task of instantly sharing his inner life with Janelle when he had never done so with anyone before. Her style made him feel not only loved and appreciated but also invaded and pressured. His tendency was to defend himself against her pushiness by withdrawal.

For Janelle, the relationship was fraught with uncertainty. She craved Bob's attention, basking in it when he gave it to her but feeling abandoned and hurt when he withdrew. The negative component of Bob's reserved and charming style was that he all too frequently needed his space from Janelle and was uncomfortable with "heart talk." When he had his fill of closeness, he wanted to be left alone. What each saw as attractive in the other also carried an undesirable side effect that neither party wanted.

This paradox is one of the most challenging aspects of any marriage. In every romantic attachment there are patterns of attraction and aversion. How partners respond to this seeming contradiction can make or break the relationship. Understanding, accepting, and working with this paradox are parts of maturing a marriage. If a couple does not face this truth and deal with it effectively, the basis of attraction becomes the cause of dissatisfaction. To effectively resolve the paradox, partners must first come to terms with the differences between what I will term *conditions* and *problems*.

Condition Versus Problem

"I never thought of it that way," Janelle exclaimed, "but I guess you're right. Bob is not going to radically change, no matter how much I want him to or how much he wants to. Accepting that he is the way he is has to be our starting point. I also want him to accept and understand me. I need attention and affection, and I don't want to become a cold, distant, or indifferent person. We will both have to learn how to work with this condition and make the best of it."

A *condition*, as a close friend frequently reminds me, is an ingrained trait you sometimes have to learn how to live with and make the best of. It is not something that quickly disappears. A *problem*, on the other hand, is something that can be solved once and for all. Relational styles such as Bob's and Janelle's are conditions, not problems. They are ingrained

ways of relating to others that have been born in the incubator
of family life and reinforced in relationship with others. They
need to be challenged and modified, but the basic styles will
remain.

Janelle will probably always want more intimacy than Bob.
She will tend to remain the initiator and caretaker, as she was
when they first met. Bob may have flashes of desire for intimate contact and learn how to initiate more closeness. He
may learn to respond better to Janelle's overtures. It is doubtful, however, that his basic orientation to relationship will
radically change. Intimacy for him will always be less comfortable and desirable than it is for Janelle. Both partners need to
work toward acceptance of their styles as a condition that
must be lived with rather than a problem that can be once and
finally fixed.

Change is possible. But change will not mean an immediate modification of style. Instead it will necessitate an ongoing
recognition of the limitations of each person's style coupled
with a commitment to working on the elements of individual
styles that can be changed to ensure each feels loved and cared
for by the other. As we shall explore, the individual changes
can lessen the relational extremes and negative feelings each
experiences while enhancing the quality of closeness and separation.

Marriage partners rarely want to deprive each other of the
love and care each needs. Serious problems can arise when the
needs of one conflict with the needs of the other. These
conflicting areas of need can be resolved if both parties resist
blame and negotiate new ways to meet each other's needs.
The first step lies in both parties understanding how their
own patterns of family closeness contribute to the current
problem. When Janelle realized that her father's neglect of her

and her caretaking of her mother drove her to pressure Bob for more love and attention, she began to modify her behavior toward Bob by admitting to her high need for attention instead of blaming him for not giving her enough. Janelle also, through counseling, stepped into her past and resolved the wounds that had accompanied her legacy of love hunger. When Bob finally admitted to himself that he didn't feel competent about expressing his emotions, he committed to participating in a men's accountability group that centered on learning how to identify feelings and communicate with women. His participation brought feelings about his past to the surface that he never realized were there. He remembered hurtful events, worked to forgive those who were involved, and started to see the blocks to his emotions dissolve.

Recognition of one's legacy of enmeshment or disengagement, and that of one's spouse, helps to diffuse the personal offense both feel. Janelle's need for intimacy conflicted with Bob's need for distance. Instead of realizing how the past controlled reactions, each tended to believe that the other was purposely being insensitive and hurtful. The resulting feeling of personal offense kept them from collaborating on how to best meet each other's needs. When they understood the roots of their condition, they began to work toward change.

Maturing Love

When first presented with the reality of a serious condition, spouses may experience a period of disappointment. Both want the unconditional, totally accepting love that marriage seemed to promise. Each wants to continue in the powerful romantic feelings of love that courtship offered, and both are more focused on their needs *for love* rather than on their responsibility *to love.*

Playwright George Bernard Shaw once wrote about romance, "When two people are under the influence of the most violent, most insane, most delusive, and most transient of passions, they are required to swear that they will stay in that excited, abnormal, and exhausting condition constantly till death do them part."

Romantic love experienced on the heels of initial attraction is powerful. It is so consuming that it blinds each to the other's negative traits. When each realizes that inherent in the attractiveness of the other person's style are undesirable side effects, romantic love wanes. Disappointment sets in and the struggle to get love escalates. In this crucial phase of marriage each must move from basing the marriage on romantic feelings to establishing a foundation of committed love.

Love is not only a feeling but also a decision. To survive the tests of time, love requires an appropriate transition from romantic feelings to sensibly permanent commitment. If this necessary transition is not made, unhealthy patterns will prevail. The struggle for getting and giving love will heighten and reinforce the negative aspects of individual style rather than the positive, affirming ones.

If Bob is unable to make a commitment to love Janelle even when he is feeling engulfed by her, he will withdraw from her and provoke the struggle even more. If Janelle is unable to release her need for his attention and commit to loving him even when he withdraws, she will contribute to the negative pattern. Each must face needs and weaknesses and make a commitment to love the other even when it hurts. Love that can extend itself to others, even when uncomfortable, is the healthy love the family and the relationship need.

It must, however, be felt and offered with the right motives to produce healthy effects.

To do so will require that each identify the dream of being perfectly loved, grieve its loss, and fashion a new, healthier dream of getting and giving love. For Janelle, that was especially hard: "My dream has always been that some tall handsome guy would fall head over heels in love with me. I remember lying in bed at night imagining him telling me how much he adored me and how special I was to him. I had such an investment in being loved. I feel sad just talking about it."

It took time for Janelle to mourn her loss and create a new dream. Bob also faced his dream of perfect love and resolved to let the unhealthy parts go and fashion a new one. Both also needed to understand what love is all about. By understanding what love is and relinquishing their "perfect partner" dreams, Bob and Janelle were re-creating a new family—enhancing their marriage and avoiding major problems later on.

Loving Rightly

The biblical concept of love is perhaps the loftiest and most demanding the world has ever known. Many of our relational patterns have evolved from Judeo-Christian beliefs and principles. The traditional Christian model of relationship involves sacrificial giving and unwavering commitment. It teaches that "it is more blessed to give than to receive" (Acts 20:35), and "greater love has no one than this, than to lay down one's life for his friends" (John 15:13).

This type of committed love makes relationships and family life thrive. Parents sacrifice for their children, denying their own needs to meet the developing needs of the children. Grown children will give up much of their time and effort to care for parents in their later years. Husbands and wives sacrifice for each other. Though this understanding of committed love has been with us for generations, much misunderstanding of its application exists.

The Bible teaches that not just one person in a relationship but both people should practice a sacrificial form of love. The model it offers for human interaction is not a give-and-take model but a give-and-give one. Each partner is to give without expecting return, making sacrifices for the other. Each is expected to push beyond comfort zones when reaching out to the other. The problems begin when only one person in the relationship takes this model to heart. One spouse will give, care, and love more than the other, creating a one-way, give-and-take dynamic within the relationship.

Give-and-take dynamics often result in the misapplication of loving feelings. The person giving, caring, or loving the other may actually be harming instead of helping the spouse. Love should always seek the best for the person being loved, but all too often a spouse who unquestionably devotes too much time, energy, and affection will inadvertently weaken the other person's character. Character is moral and ethical strength. Indulging another's needs and shortcomings weakens the desire and ability to do what is right. The love, care, and concern that everyone needs should be balanced with challenge, sacrifice, and difficulty. Being on the receiving end of excessive care takes the pressure off what makes a person grow. The one who gives less becomes less. One-way loving must be closely scrutinized to assure it is not too lavish and harmful to the other's growth.

We must examine our motive for loving. Sacrificial love blesses us and others when our motive is truly sacrificial. If we give love to get, however, the love won't work. Healthy sacrificial love affirms, values, and encourages others. It also challenges them to take care of themselves in healthy ways. The maturing of love requires not only that we commit to love each other but also that we do it rightly.

Handling the Need for Love

Research has shown that contrary to many people's perspective, happiness comes as a by-product of right living but is elusive when pursued as a goal in and of itself. When one pursues happiness as a goal, failure and disappointment frequently follow. Fulfillment in marriage works on the same principle. To work through the normal disappointments and struggles of being loved, partners must focus on their responsibilities rather than their needs. Each will be fulfilled in responsibly loving the other. Being preoccupied with being loved brings only torment.

Focusing on responsibilities, however, does not mean ignoring needs. We all need love, attention, affection, affirmation, and acceptance. Emotional needs must be recognized and evaluated. Many needs are powerful because they have been fueled by the rejections and wounds of childhood. To expect a spouse to meet these needs is tantamount to requiring the spouse to heal the wound. Needs should not be turned into demands and expectations of others. Rather, they should be reviewed in light of the past and surrendered to God for healing and fulfillment. Surrendering deepest needs to God for His healing touch and ongoing affirmation can bring peace to the inner being.

The Gatewoods came to see me, and Bob related an experience from his men's commitment group: "I was telling my group how my mother rarely paid attention to me when I got teary eyed and could hardly talk. Everybody waited for me to say more, but I couldn't. I sat there not saying a thing. It was like a tight band was around my throat and chest. Jerry, the group leader, came over and hugged me from the back, and then the dam burst. When I felt his arms around me, I started to heave and sob like I never have before. He prayed that I would feel Jesus' arms loving me, making up for all the times my mom and dad never put their arms around me. Something lifted that night. I can only say now that I feel different. I feel more loved and able to love."

Wounds come from the unmet needs of the past and also of the present. Living in a relationship that is currently not meeting needs for love can be very wounding. Janelle was continually feeling wounded by Bob's lack of response. She needed healing of her past and relief in the present.

If you are feeling the hurt of not being loved the way you need to be, offer your pain to God. Reach out to Him. The love hunger within can be satiated when you partake of His goodness and experience His touch. An intimate relationship with God will fulfill the deep need for perfect love, acceptance, and attachment. When you fill your need with God first, adding people, places, and things to your life will enrich you instead of draining you.

Overcoming the Roadblocks to Change

Your first steps in making your marriage work reside in your ability to understand and deal with the way the legacies of family closeness are played out in the marital relationship. As you recognize the positives and negatives of your style of relating, you are then able to commit to a more mature love of your spouse.

Making this transition may be difficult for many couples for the following reasons:

- The partners lack an understanding of the paradox of attraction. They are unable to see that what attracts them to each other also may eventually repel them. Most think that the other person, rather than the pattern, is the problem.

- Partners fail to accept their differences as a condition to be worked with and adjusted to rather than a problem that can be quickly solved. Basic styles of relating probably won't change dramatically. However, each partner needs an ongoing recognition of the limitations of style and a commitment to reach beyond the comfort zone to help meet the needs of the loved one.

- The couple may not fully realize that a transition from romantic love to committed love is necessary in all marriage relationships. Few will consciously make a decision to love sacrificially. Many of those who do love and care are loving for the wrong reasons. Each will need to examine the need for love as well as the commitment to love.

- Both individuals will need to step back into the past, examine their family legacies, and challenge the unhealthy dreams and patterns that have resulted. The wounds that empower the love hunger and unhealthy patterns must be healed. These wounds provoke people to be too protective of self or seek love from others too ardently. Though wounds may not be healed instantaneously, their effects can be diminished. The dreams of being loved perfectly by another must be released and refashioned.

In the next chapter, we will examine how to make marriage work by making intimacy work. Doing so will help to refine the steps that bring a workable resolve to the struggle over closeness. Partners need to embrace an intimate and healthy style of relationship to make the marriage work well. When intimacy works, the family flourishes—re-creation is going on.

CHAPTER 7

Negotiating Closeness

We are amphibious. We are created to bear
both separateness and closeness. It is only
when we bring these two capacities together
that we experience true intimacy.
—Donald Durham

Intimacy is the touching of two souls, the joining of two
spirits. It is the profound experience of two individuals sharing the innermost being with each other. The feeling of intimacy is powerfully enriching. When we taste it, something in
the inner being is affected. We are less alone, less pained, and
seemingly more whole. We feel deeply touched and renewed.
It is what all of us, especially love hungry individuals, seem to
want but rarely get.

Intimacy requires vulnerability. To experience its riches,
one must lower barriers, become transparent, and open up the
secret inner chambers of hidden thought and feeling. This can

make the pursuit of intimacy an approach-avoidance conflict, something that is both desired and feared. The enmeshed individual wants intimacy and fears not being loved in return. The disengaged individual desires its enrichment but fears the required vulnerability. Though both desire the enhanced feelings of love that intimacy brings, neither will find fulfillment easily. The enmeshed spouse, who has a greater desire for closeness, will push for intimacy; but the more one spouse pressures the other, the more threatening the situation may seem, encouraging a climate of avoidance. Bob and Janelle Gatewood struggled with intimacy in this way.

"I don't want to be close all the time," Bob declared. "Janelle pushes and pushes for us to talk, and it gets really irritating after a while. If she would leave me alone, I would probably want to talk to her more."

Bob's resentment of Janelle's push for closeness is common to individuals with disengaged orientations. From Bob's point of view, the total sharing of his innermost being was not an easy or necessarily attractive thing to do. Bob, at times, felt overwhelmed and invaded by Janelle. He remained distant to avoid the anxious feeling her pressure for closeness provoked. Being close stirred his fears of engulfment. He also resisted her demands for closeness because giving in would open his deeply personal thoughts and feelings to exposure.

Exposure of the inner life is especially threatening to a disengaged person. The lack of closeness from the past makes him suspicious of what someone will do with his tender inner feelings. His protective boundaries are well established and rigid. Only on rare occasions and if the climate for sharing is absolutely safe will he let down the barriers and open up his heart.

"Bob is adamantly closed to sharing what he feels or

thinks with me," Janelle reported. "I get so frustrated and hurt. What is a marriage if it isn't the sharing of two lives? We live like two acquaintances."

An enmeshed individual desires a lot of closeness. She wants to recapture the rich feeling of shared intimacy from childhood. If she is denied it, she feels tormented.

Janelle was frustrated and hurt by her lack of intimacy with Bob. She felt something was missing unless she was close to him. She also felt deeply rejected when he didn't respond. Those feelings motivated her to put too much pressure for intimacy on her husband.

Both partners' conditioning created an imbalance that only worsened with time. Janelle's fear that Bob would not love her caused her to pursue him too intensely, just as Bob's fears caused him to avoid closeness too much.

Both Janelle and Bob need the balance of healthy intimacy. To really work, intimacy needs to become the by-product of a healthy relationship, not its sole goal. The more one pursues it, the more elusive it can be. Wounded hearts either cry out for it or avoid it because of their deep love hunger from the past. As children, Bob and Janelle did not have honest and transparent, caring and accepting relationships with their parents. No one was lovingly intimate with them. If closeness was present, it wasn't a healthy intimacy with age-appropriate sharing.

Intimacy requires the foundation of a healthy relationship. Transparency, vulnerability, and acceptance are necessary for intimacy to work, but so are separateness and distance. Intimacy emanates from a personal ability to embrace closeness fully and to allow separation or distance without anxiety. Enmeshed individuals can experience profuse amounts of closeness but are too dependent on it and suffer anxiety when they do not have it. Disengaged individuals can easily tolerate separateness and distance but fear being too close. The struggle over intimacy can be greatly lessened if both face their fears.

The Fears

Fear is a powerful motivator. The Bible makes a significant comment about fear when it says, "Fear involves torment" (1 John 4:18). Few emotional states are more distressing than the constellation of fear, worry, and anxiety. Individuals experiencing distress in a relationship often have no idea what a big role fear plays. Over and over again in my counseling, I have watched people become literally dumbfounded when I tell them they are fearful. Like Janelle and Bob, people tend to be more in touch with their frustration, hurt, or anger than with their fear; but deep within each of us, fear motivates and empowers patterns of action and reaction. This makes fear one of the most hurtful legacies of a background of intense disengagement or enmeshment.

Disengaged individuals fear closeness in part because it is so foreign to their experience. Because no parent closely bonded with them or intimately cared for their feelings or the deep inner fears common to childhood, they have come to trust only their own ways of caring for themselves. They do not trust that others will rightly care for the inner being. In families, this lack creates havoc, not health! As adults, they fear risking the needed vulnerability, and they lack the trust required to experience another's intimate care and concern. Fear is at the root of their distancing; yet if asked, most will argue that they have no need for intimacy. Unable to see the fear that empowers their avoidance, they will say, "I just don't need closeness that much."

Individuals from enmeshed backgrounds experience the torment of fear when intimacy is not returned. A side effect of the lavish closeness of their childhood is a feeling of uneasiness when not connected to another. These individuals are too dependent on feelings of closeness. Additionally, their understanding of what love is all about stems from their experience of enmeshment in childhood.

Janelle recalled starting her day as a preteen by sitting on her mom's bed discussing her goals for the day while her mom ate breakfast. When returning from school, she rushed to her mom's bedside eager to share the events of the day. Janelle expected similar intimate encounters with Bob. When they were not forthcoming in her marriage, she worried that Bob may not love her. Individuals from enmeshed backgrounds worry a lot about getting or losing the love or relationship they so depend on, or they worry that it will be all their fault if the relationship doesn't work. The worry will prompt them to love, care, or give too much and pressure too much for intimate connection.

Both partners must understand their patterns and address their fears, recognizing their deep-seated roots, before change is possible. Though the symptoms of fear can vary from person to person, torment, anxiety, avoidance feelings, doubt, confusion, and worry are all expressions of fear. These feelings are so negative, people create defensive or offensive responses to avoid them. Disengaged people will feel uncomfortable and cornered when confronted with these emotions. Enmeshed people will pursue closeness with a vengeance in hopes of assuaging anxiety. Both responses are self-defeating.

To conquer the fears and properly negotiate closeness, each must recognize the root of fear that is empowering the negative pattern. Without recognition of the root, no healing or change is possible. Like the root of a felled tree, the tree will regrow because nourishment is still being offered by the roots.

Both must also openly admit to their fears. Change is possible when they take full responsibility for what they need to change. Open admission of what needs change empowers individuals because they are better able to take ownership of shortcomings. Once recognized, the fears must be argued against. Fear can be described as *False Expectations Appearing Real*. Truth brings fear into proper perspective. A disengaged individual is not going to be totally engulfed by his partner. He won't be devastated by opening his heart to another. An enmeshed person is not going to be denied personal fulfillment because of a lack of love. She can learn how to live happily without being close all the time.

Finally, the wound of the past that created the fear must be healed. A parent who does not bond rightly with a child has wounded the child's inner being, setting the stage for future unhealthy relational patterns. Even if the parent did it unwittingly, the wound must be recognized, thoroughly examined, forgiven, and submitted to God's love for healing. Chapter 12 offers guidance for healing wounds from the past.

Creating New Patterns

Facing fear releases the marriage from the bondage of the past. It enables each partner to negotiate a new relationship of closeness based on what is healthy. Doing so requires an understanding of different styles of marriage. Marriage styles are a composite of the relationship and role patterns of each partner. To meet the need for closeness in a healthy manner, one needs to know how a healthy marriage should work. If there is no appropriate standard to aim for, each person will craft a different type of intimacy, possibly re-creating another unhealthy pattern from the past.

Remember our previous example of Archie and Edith Bunker? They illustrate the *traditional marriage* most prevalent in the 1940s and 1950s. Many of our parents exemplified this style of marriage. Dad was the head of the home and Mom the heart. Dad was responsible for breadwinning, and he retained the final word on all major decisions. Mom raised the children, took care of the home, and had primary responsibility for making the marriage and family relationships work. That style of marriage had clearly defined roles for each partner, which created stability and predictability, but it also had problems. It lacked intimacy and collaboration in the marriage. It made for poor bonding patterns between Dad and the kids and Mom and the kids.

Like Archie Bunker, my dad often relied too heavily on being authoritarian, seeing himself as the boss who knew best. He also tended to remain distant and disengaged from the kids because he left all the parenting tasks to Mom. As many fathers did, he used authority as a defense against closeness and vulnerability.

Mom was the partner who pushed for intimacy and closeness, at the same time being careful not to pressure Dad too much so that he wouldn't get mad. She openly deferred to Dad but manipulated family life behind the scenes. Like Edith, she tried to protect us and herself from his demands. She took too much responsibility for the well-being of the family, often acting as the go-between. She met her emotional needs through her children rather than Dad, which fostered our enmeshment with her and our disengagement from Dad.

The answer to healthy marital and familial closeness is not found in the relational patterns of the traditional marriage. Though this marriage style is often a very stable one, it is rarely emotionally fulfilling for either partner. The patterns of parenting and emotional caretaking found in a traditional marriage are ultimately unhealthy for the children, fostering unhealthy patterns in them.

Another style of marriage, called the *bartered marriage,* developed when children from traditional families of the 1940s and 1950s experimented with new styles of marriage in the sixties and seventies. The woman feared being dominated as her mother had been. She did not prize intimacy as much as her mother had, and she wanted equality instead. The man usually went along because he didn't want to be perceived as domineering like his father. This type of marriage also freed him from having to assume the total responsibility for breadwinning that his father carried. Everything from housework to breadwinning was bartered by the couple. Some men tried being househusbands, while many wives assumed career tracks.

Though an attempt at creating new and possibly healthier ways of relating, this style often suffers because it is based too much on performance and conditional love. The requisite sacrifices of healthy closeness compete with the bartered demands, and often lose. The stability of the traditional marriage is lacking, and bonding patterns with the children are also uncertain due to bartering. Even though more equality is stressed, intimacy and closeness suffer. Both partners are too protective of themselves, and neither is able to surrender to the vulnerability that intimacy and closeness require. Many individuals who practice this style of marriage end up disillusioned. They have worked out a good system of fairness, but they lack the intimacy that adds zest and meaning to a marriage.

In recent times the *reversed marriage* style has gained popularity. In this style of relationship the husband may still be the breadwinner, but he is passive in every other respect. The direction and decision making of the family rest firmly with the wife, who refuses to be a doormat like Edith. Janelle and Bob Gatewood's marriage evolved into a reversed marriage style.

"I run the house, raise the kids, and pay the bills," Janelle asserted. "Bob works, but that's all he does. He won't lift a finger at home or help me with the kids unless I make him. You'd think he would see what needs to be done around the house without me telling him!"

Janelle contributed most of the thought and energy required to make the family run smoothly. She even worked part-time as a pool nurse to help out with the bills. Typical of the husband in most reversed marriages, Bob did not seem to reciprocate, no matter how much effort his wife put in. He responded to her if she nagged, but he rarely initiated any activities of his own around the house.

"It gets old when she complains all the time. If she would leave me alone, I would do more," Bob lamented. "Janelle pushes, nags, and bosses so much that I find myself resenting her. It makes it that much harder for me to want to do anything to help."

The push-pull struggle over closeness has extended into the entire marriage relationship. Neither partner is experiencing the desired level of intimacy. Janelle's overfunctioning is not improving the marriage relationship or their family life. Bob's passivity and withdrawal are harmful. Both are settling into parallel lives lacking closeness and tied together through routine. The children will suffer from the parents' lack of marital resolve because Bob will remain disengaged from the children and Janelle will remain enmeshed with them. Like the traditional marriage, the reversed marriage does not produce healthy marital and familial closeness.

The One-Flesh Marriage

The previous styles of marriage lack appropriate intimacy, balanced responsibilities, personal fulfillment, or all three. Each style, as we shall see in Part 4, also creates negative responses in the children. The *one-flesh marriage* style, however, offers a healthy model of balanced fulfillment. In this style the roles and relationships are not individually negotiated. Neither are they created from the wounds of the past; rather, the roles and patterns of relationship are developed from biblical guidelines and the partners' consciences before God. The frame of reference for responding to each other is developed out of studied effort and conviction rather than personal preference and wounding.

Ward Keller, a friend of mine who brought his marriage from the brink of despair to wholeness, shared with me what he learned about the one-flesh marriage style: "I see myself as responsible for the physical, financial, emotional, and spiritual needs of my family. The buck stops with me. That doesn't mean I create all the problems, but it does mean I will take responsibility to settle them. If I'm the leader of my family, then just like the CEO of any organization, I have the ultimate responsibility of making sure the marriage and relationships work."

As Ward explained, the one-flesh style requires the husband to take responsibility for more than the physical needs of his family. He must also commit himself to meeting the emotional and relational needs of his wife and children. He is neither a dictatorial leader nor a passive doormat. He is a sacrificial leader who provides direction through example, collaboration, and problem solving with his wife.

The wife sees her role as coequally responsible for the needs of the family. She is neither a doormat nor a controller.

The partners in a one-flesh marriage are best described as a team of two individuals who desire God's will for their marriage, family, and lives. As an acquaintance of mine is fond of saying, "To make a marriage work, spouses do not give 50 percent and 50 percent; they give 100 percent and 100 percent." The husband is the managing partner or team leader. The wife is cofounder and colaborer. Both are committed to unity of effort and action. Both acknowledge their responsibility to each other and to God for how they conduct their marriage, lives, and relationships.

When both individuals in a marriage commit to such a partnership, oneness results. Oneness is not about dominating or being dominated. It is not about sameness. Rather, it is unity through right cooperation of different parts based on each partner's strengths and weaknesses. The goal of marriage is the complementary unification of two distinctly different individuals into a healthy working team. This goal challenges each partner to commit to something bigger and better than either. Negotiating closeness is necessary to produce a viable team. The two members need to overcome their differing needs for closeness and create a relationship that fosters both intimacy and separateness.

Intimate, Yet Separate

A person with an enmeshed orientation has difficulty with separateness and depends on being closely connected. It is scary to be disconnected from a loved one. A person from a disengaged background experiences the opposite, being used to separateness and wanting to avoid being close for too long. Negotiating closeness requires that both resolve their fears and work toward change. The basic tendencies may remain the same, but the conflicting extremes can be lessened.

The growing edge for an enmeshed individual is to learn how to be comfortable without being intimately connected to another. The person needs to complete the emotional process of individuation. The person needs to learn how to be a self-contained individual who can be comfortable when intimate and close as well as when separate and distant. It's good to desire intimacy but not to the point that its absence provokes torment or control. The goal of change for an enmeshed person is to eliminate the torment and the demand for intimacy without becoming disengaged and hard-hearted. An enmeshed individual did not rightly experience the childhood transition from closeness to separateness and is still stuck in the past, wanting to re-create the closeness that was present but never provided in a healthy way.

The disengaged individual, on the other hand, prizes independence too much, using it as a justification for the lack of closeness. The individual has become too focused on personal comfort and safety, fearing to risk or accept mutual responsibility for closeness. The person needs to learn how to connect emotionally and remain vulnerable—to be trusting and intimate. The growing edge is to resist the temptation to withdraw when intimate connection is offered or pressured for.

The inner feelings of panic and resistance must be overcome so that both intimacy and distance can be enjoyable.

To check where you may be in regard to your ability to be intimate, yet separate, answer the following questions:

- When your spouse doesn't pay attention to you for periods of time, do you become hurt, angry, or tormented? Or are you able to relax and let it go?

- When your spouse desires closeness and intimacy, do you feel uncomfortable and push away? Or are you able to cheerfully respond?

- Have both separation and closeness become familiar and easy?

Steps to Healthy Intimacy

Enmeshed and disengaged tendencies can be lessened, and healthy intimacy and separateness can be developed. This, I believe, is the work of marriage that most couples face. It requires each person to work on accepting the other while changing himself or herself. It also requires communication and negotiation.

The commitment and the ability to negotiate closeness are characteristics of a re-created marriage and family. To do so requires that each partner change to some degree. If the push-pull struggle is powerful and frustrating, as was Janelle and Bob Gatewood's, the assistance of a counselor may be necessary. The following steps will also help.

Both Partners Must Recognize the Push-Pull Pattern and Their Contribution to It

Janelle recognized and admitted to her tormenting need for closeness while Bob came to believe that he was deficient in relating intimately to another. Both were able to shift from blaming the other person to recognizing the hurtful pattern and understanding how each contributed. Being able to shift from blame to ownership is a major challenge. During one of our sessions, Bob expressed how he felt the problem was really Janelle's, not his: "If she wouldn't push so much and be angry all the time, we would get along great." Janelle countered, "If you would just pay attention to me and not withdraw into your own little world, everything would be fine!"

For the Gatewoods, it took a third party to demonstrate each partner's contribution. This shift can also occur when a couple come to realize that their current situation is not new but a pattern already developed and practiced in the past. When Bob realized that the disengagement of his childhood formed the emotional scaffolding of his adult life, he was able to admit to his deficiencies and stop blaming Janelle. Similarly, Janelle stopped blaming Bob when she recognized how her family legacy of enmeshment was influencing the marriage. Though it is ideal for both to recognize the need to change, one partner's awareness and commitment to change the pattern can also help. When one stops pushing, the other lessens the pulling away.

Each Must Step Back into the Past and Resolve the Fears, Wounds, and Dreams That Have Empowered the Pattern

"My fears of being close to Janelle were tied to my childhood, but I didn't believe what you told me until I had that experience in the men's group," Bob confessed. Fears are hard for disengaged people to recognize and harder still for enmeshed individuals to release. Both, with God's help, stepped back into the past and found healing for their wounds and fears. They were also able to identify the unrealistic dreams of their deficient childhoods and mourn their losses. Facing the past, being healed of the wounds, and working through the grief of losses release the power of the past on the present. Dying to the dreams of what each envisioned as perfect love freed the Gatewoods to forge a more realistic picture of how to love each other in the present. (See Chapter 12 for how to resolve wounds from the past.)

The Couple Must Adopt a Healthy Style of Marriage Based on Studied Effort and Personal Conviction

The Gatewoods committed to attend a Sunday school class on marriage. At first Bob dragged his feet but, after attending a few times, found that he had a lot in common with other men in the class. Janelle had always been a willing attendee, pushing for Bob's participation as well as his cooperation in reading books and listening to tapes. Bob viewed her past efforts as attempts to show him how wrong he was and how right she had always been. Once Janelle stopped blaming him, Bob was ready to read books and listen to tapes because he knew it wasn't all going to be his fault.

Study aids add new information that can help couples discuss and decide on a better course of action. Our counseling center stocks a large supply of books and audio and video tapes that specifically deal with how to make marriage and family life work. These aids offer insights and practical steps to challenging the old patterns and fashioning new ones.

Each Must Commit to Remain Both Closely and Intimately Connected While Allowing for Times of Separation and Reduced Connection

A balance of closeness and distance must be agreed upon to allow both parties to get and give love in healthy ways. Janelle's preoccupation with closeness must be balanced with healthy distance. For Bob, the opposite is true. When the partners agree that both ends of the spectrum have value, it is no longer a power struggle to see who is going to get his or her way. When there is agreement to accept both aspects of relationship, both individuals win.

Once the commitment was made, Janelle immediately questioned, "How are we going to know when to be separate and when to be intimate? Who determines this?" True to form, the one who has pursued relationship the most will usually want the most clarity on when to be close. The next step involves communication and negotiation.

The Couple Must Learn How to Communicate and Resolve Conflict Effectively

The ability to communicate well and resolve conflict is a learned skill. Susan and I, as well as most couples I know, have difficulty with communication. One partner doesn't want to talk while the other seems to chatter incessantly. Failure to communicate is the number-one stated reason for divorce.

Resolving conflict is a skill that can be taught and learned by anyone, regardless of personality type. I answered Janelle's question of who was to determine the times of closeness and distance by saying, "The two of you must negotiate this by learning conflict resolution skills."

When the power of the patterns has been reduced and blame transformed to ownership, the couple is ready to negotiate a new pattern of giving and getting love. I had Bob and Janelle sit in chairs opposite each other, and I began to teach them how to resolve conflict. First, we adopted a model for resolving conflict that required each to take turns sharing and listening. I taught Janelle how to share by attacking the problem instead of Bob. As she shared, Bob listened—but not like he used to. This kind of listening is called active listening. He was required to be nondefensive and only ask her questions and summarize what he heard her say. After Janelle fully shared her heart on an issue and Bob was able to understand it, they switched roles; Bob shared while Janelle listened. The practice of structured sharing and listening taught them the skills to work out ways to manage their closeness and separateness.

Janelle reported, "Each time I feel like Bob has been too distant for too long, I ask him to set aside a time when we can talk. He then chooses a time, and we share. The sharing can get pretty hot, but when it does, we stop and try it again later. We've had a few big fights that took us four different rounds of stopping and starting again before we resolved the issues. It's hard work, but it's worth it. And Bob thinks so, too."

Passing On the Patterns

As I have described previously, deficient patterns of love that are not conquered in one generation are passed on to the next. Unresolved and unhealthy patterns of closeness or distance are destined to repeat themselves in future generations. One result of unresolved issues of closeness and unhealthy marriage styles can be the creation of surrogate roles for the children. Simply put, a surrogate is a substitute.

When a husband and a wife cannot resolve their conflicts and successfully meet each other's needs, the temptation is to find something or someone else to meet that need. In many marriages the wife feels she does not receive the love or attention her husband should provide. As a result, she finds fulfillment through her children. She may have one child in whom she confides. Responding to her need and the attention she gives, the child slowly takes over the role of emotional caretaking and becomes a surrogate, or substitute spouse.

In Part 4, we will explore in more depth how generational strongholds of mismanaged love and intimacy affect parenting patterns and result in relational problems for the children when they reach adulthood. The result is an unhealthy family that perpetuates destructive patterns of love. Re-creating a marriage is perhaps the most elemental step to re-creating family—it provides the nurture, love, and care required to grow healthy children who can give and get love appropriately.

PART 4

FASHIONING OUR CHILDREN'S LEGACY

Parents are thermostats and children thermometers. Our children can best show us who we are and what's happening in the family. How we manage our marriages, personal problems, and need fulfillment will shape who our children become, the problems they may experience, how they will parent their children, and what type of families they will create.

CHAPTER 8

Partner or Parent?

The most important thing a father can do for his children is to love their mother.
—Theodore Hesburgh

Bill Lewis, a salesman for a major electronics firm, had an odd combination of surface southern charm and an underlying reserve and seriousness. When I first met Bill and his wife, Kay, at one of our Family Week programs, they struck me as a troubled couple. Kay was very open and quite willing to share on a personal level. Bill and their daughter Bonnie were much more remote. As I watched the family, I noticed that though Bonnie looked like her dad, she was obviously closer to her mother. She rarely interacted with Bill, and when they did talk, it was mostly one-sided—a reprimand from Bill.

Early in the week when I spoke on family patterns, Kay approached me to discuss her immediate concerns. "I didn't realize what I was doing until you pointed it out," she said. "Bill was gone so much of the time it was natural for me to spend more and more of my time with Bonnie. She's always been so caring and sensitive to my needs. She told me when she was only four and a half that she loved me and would take care of me when she grew up. It never occurred to me that we might be too close. But truthfully, I enjoy her company more than her dad's!"

Twelve-year-old Bonnie desired to please her mother more than anyone else. By contrast, Kay's marital relationship with Bill was distant and difficult. Bill traveled a lot and was insensitive to Kay's needs when he was at home. My concern for Kay, however, was not only for the health of her marriage but also for her enmeshment with Bonnie. If she did not deal with the situation soon, she would continue the same hurtful patterns of her childhood. As I later found out when I got to know them better, both she and Bill were living out their family bonding legacies, unaware of how the legacies affected their marriage and in turn their child's future relationship patterns.

A Surrogate Spouse

Bonnie was Kay's surrogate or substitute spouse. Kay fulfilled the emotional needs that weren't being met in her marriage in an inappropriately close relationship with her daughter Bonnie. Just as she had been her father's intimate friend, so she made Bonnie her constant companion. When a parent invests too many emotional needs in a child, the child becomes a substitute partner, sharing the parent's burdens and joys much as a marriage partner would. The boundaries of discretion, authority, and caring between the parent and the child are not as firm as they should be. Mom will share thoughts and feelings with the child that are more appropriate for an adult relationship. The child will respond wholeheartedly to Mom's investment, enjoying the rich reward of her intimacy. The child appears to thrive in this relational culture, but it is eventually harmful to the child, who needs to be parented, not partnered.

Boundaries

Boundaries are the dividing lines between people, helping individuals define themselves in relation to others. A dictionary definition of a *boundary* is "a line that marks the outermost extent of an area, or a division between areas." Personal boundaries help us relate to others in a healthy manner. Healthy boundaries help us take appropriate responsibility for ourselves as well as others. They are extremely important for emotional well-being. Boundaries clarify the following questions:

- What are my rights as a person?

- What are your rights as a person?

- Who am I in relation to you?

- What are my responsibilities to you?

- What are your responsibilities to me?

- Who makes decisions for me?

- Who makes decisions for you?

When a son or daughter is partnered instead of parented, boundaries become confusing to the child. The most common result is for the child to take on the responsibility of nurturing and protecting the parent instead of receiving nurture and protection. The child will neglect self and become too responsible for the parent's emotional well-being. The deep tendency within every child to idolize a parent encourages this inclination. The child learns the role of caretaker of Mom's or Dad's emotional needs. The child hopes to make up for the parent's hurt, disappointment, or loss by comforting and pleasing the parent.

A child who must comfort a sad parent is not in a good position to learn how to resolve her own feelings. Bonnie learned how to carry Kay's sadness but not her own. When a child learns to comfort in this manner, it is always at her expense. When she grows up, her tendency to comfort others will be too well developed. She will adopt a caretaking role in marriage and other relationships, having difficulty saying no to someone else's needs. She must learn to recognize her needs and resist taking too much responsibility for the emotional needs of others.

Being partnered instead of parented can also produce the opposite effect in a child. The child may expect others to take care of him when it would be more appropriate for him to take care of himself, and this expectation can extend into adulthood. Jack Hunsinger, a tall athlete, was experiencing difficulty in his marriage due to the surrogate role he lived out in childhood.

During a counseling session, his wife, Katrina, explained the problem: "Jack expects me to take care of him just like his mother did. He wants me to do everything for him, from picking up his clothes to making him feel better if he's depressed. It doesn't matter how tired I am. His needs always come first. I can't keep taking care of him and three kids, too."

Jack was very close to his divorced mother, who had always favored him over his sister and treated him more like a partner than a child. Unlike Bonnie Lewis's mother, Kay, who expected Bonnie to take care of her, Jack's mother got her needs met in the relationship by being overly caring and helpful to Jack. She spoiled him.

This type of surrogate role produces a child like Jack who expects others to comfort and care for him. When the parent is overly indulgent of the child's emotions, the child will expect Mom, Dad, and others to cater to his feelings. The child thinks that he comes first and everyone else second. The parent's need for intimate relationship with the child causes the relationship to be conducted on the child's terms. This is obviously unhealthy for the child.

Surrogate roles can place either too much emphasis on the child caring for the parent or too much emphasis on the parent caring for the child. A parent's role should be one of instruction and support, not pleasing and excessive care. Finding this balance requires diligence; few parents realize when they are partnering instead of parenting. It is a great temptation for a lonely or unfulfilled parent to be appreciative of the care, love, and concern the child shows. Perhaps the child is the only one offering the love, attention, or intimacy the parent so desperately needs.

Ironically, while the child is fulfilling this role, others may commend the parent on having such a caring child. Kay Lewis's friends frequently commented on how much they admired the close relationship she had with her daughter Bonnie. In the face of such affirmation, the parent may not realize how destructive the relationship can be to the child. The serious harm done by this kind of relationship should not be underestimated.

"I'm still in shock," Kay lamented. "Not only was I too close to Bonnie, but I think I was too close to my dad. It never occurred to me that a parent could be too close to a child."

Kay's awareness led to a gradual distancing from Bonnie, which started her on the road to healthy autonomy. She and Bill continued in marriage counseling until their struggle over intimacy was improved. If the partnering had not been challenged and changed, Bonnie might have ended up with the same problem that Mark LeBaron experienced.

Arrested Development

The enmeshment of a child with one or both parents can result in the child's inability to pursue his destiny in life. Mark LeBaron was having great difficulty finding and pursuing a dream of fulfillment for his life. Trudy LeBaron, his mother, came to me for advice. She was plagued with worry over her son's lack of direction.

"Mark is so bright. His scores were extremely high on his college admission test, yet he still hasn't finished school and isn't doing anything with his life," Trudy explained. "He's living with me because he doesn't have anywhere else to go. I don't know how I can help him. I'm so worried about him. We have always been close. It tears me up to see my thirty-year-old son so lost."

Trudy was worried about her grown son's inability to find a niche in life. His father had died when Mark was young, and Trudy had raised him by herself. The two of them had always been the best of friends, but now the more she spoke to him about life issues, the farther apart they became. Unknown to both, the result of their partnering was becoming manifest.

A study done on men who flunked out of Harvard University after their first year highlighted another negative result of parental partnering. The students who failed had entrance exam scores and high-school grade point averages similar to others who had not failed. Puzzled at first, researchers discovered a striking difference when they looked at the students' family dynamics. It appeared that those who flunked out were different from those who remained in one key characteristic—the ones who failed were too closely bonded to their mothers. All too often college life was for them the opportunity to become what their mothers had envisioned they could become. They were not truly living out the pursuit of their dreams, and they failed to develop personal motivation once they were away from the mother's daily influence. This lack of personal goal orientation is termed *destiny malaise,* an inability to grasp hold of one's destiny.

Some people struggle with discovering and living out their life ambitions instead of fulfilling their parents' desires and dreams. As in Mark LeBaron's case, the surrogate partnering hampers personal development, blocking the ability of even the best and the brightest to become productive members of society. The boundary confusion of a surrogate relationship creates an inability in children, when grown, to know what they truly desire. Having been so tuned in to the parent's needs and ambitions, they have never gained sight of self. As adults, they struggle with finding out who they are and what they were destined to accomplish.

Trudy needed to let go of Mark and stop pressuring him to fulfill her expectations. Much of the answer to an adult child's destiny malaise lies in the parent's willingness to let go of the need to help the adult child find the path through life. Once the voice of his mother was quieted, Mark was able to develop his own inner voice of guidance and direction. It took a few years and it was hard for Trudy to let go, but Mark finally got a job with a small computer hardware company.

The Wound of Defrauding

The word *defraud* means "to be cheated out of something that is rightfully yours." Sons or daughters who are surrogate spouses for the parent of the opposite sex are defrauded. They are cheated out of healthy parenting, and perhaps more important, they are emotionally cheated in ways they do not understand.

Mothers and Sons

Brian Morrison worked as a contract house painter. He and his wife had gotten a divorce. During a therapy session, he shared his newfound understanding of the dynamic of defrauding: "My dad and mom always had problems. Dad was never around when any of us needed him. He spent most of his life on a bar stool with his cronies. I guess you could say that I became the man of the house. I always tried to protect Mom and help her out whenever possible. I didn't want Dad to hurt her anymore. It was only after Paula divorced me that I realized how protective and possessive I had also been of her."

When a son is too close to his mother for too long, becoming her substitute spouse, it stirs his natural desires to protect and possess. Because he is not his mother's husband, both of these unconscious desires will be thwarted. He will not be able to protect her to the full extent of his desire. Obviously, short of incest, he will also not be able to sexually possess her. This can result in an inner emotional response of feeling defrauded. The intimacy invited by his mother is never consummated, and the protectiveness is never fully realized. When a desire is frustrated in this manner, it often grows in strength. As an adult, the son will relate to women in highly protective and sexual ways.

Brian's problem with his wife, Paula, also included adultery: "Paula and I battled over sex all the time. At the beginning of our marriage, we had sex every day, and she didn't seem to mind. It just seemed like every time I'd get close to her, I would want to have sex with her. But after a while she turned me down more and more. Now I realize I really didn't want just sex, I wanted closeness."

Brian's problems were directly related to his bonding patterns with his mother. He was attempting to re-create the protective and intimate feelings of his childhood while consummating the desires he had never fully acted on. The result was a style of relating that was possessive and controlling as well as sexual. All Brian really wanted was a close and loving family, but his unhealthy relational style made his wife feel suffocated, driving her farther and farther from him.

A second aspect of defrauding manifests itself in the child's relationship with his father, his stepfather, or the other significant man in his mother's life. The emotional connectedness he experiences with his mother puts him in direct competition with the other man.

Brian's feelings are common to most men who have experienced this type of defrauding in childhood: "There's a lot about Dad I don't like, especially the way he treated my mother. We have always been on opposite sides of the fence. I only talk to him now because Mom wants me to. He doesn't go out of his way to give me the time of day and never has."

When someone is left out, a triangle will result. Two individuals compete for the attention of a third, and one loses. In surrogate spouse relationships, this competition can create conflict as it did for Brian; yet rarely do the participants realize what is actually happening. Even if one of them senses the dynamic, he will rarely confront and overcome it. This is especially true of the husband. He feels cheated of his wife's attention since so much of it goes to the child. His unconscious tendency is to become embittered and to try to get even, often punishing the child for his wife's overinvolvement. The most common form of punishment is an attitude of coldness and distance toward the child; in essence, he is saying to the enmeshed spouse, "If you want the kid so bad, take him. He's all yours!"

Another common response is to become critical of the child, focusing on his weaknesses in hopes of creating distance between him and the enmeshed parent. The child always suffers when parents don't resolve their marital conflict.

Fathers and Daughters

A similar pattern emerges when the father is enmeshed in a substitute spousal role with his daughter. As with the mother-son scenario, this creates problems of defrauding. The daughter will be in competition with her mother for Dad's affections. She will either experience conflict with her mother or be very cold and distant toward her, resulting in little bonding between them. The daughter may also experience destiny malaise, creating difficulty when she must make the transition from Dad's expectations to her own.

Remember Bonnie's mother, Kay Lewis? She was her

dad's surrogate spouse while growing up. In her adult relationships she vied for the attention of men. The intimate need for involvement with Dad created a love hunger in her for the same close involvement with other men. She had difficulty living without a man in her life and found it far easier to make friendships with men than with women. Because her father felt negatively toward her mother, she took on those negative judgments and generalized them toward all women. Having failed to learn how to be intimate and comfortable with members of her own sex, she had few, if any, satisfying relationships with other women. However, she easily made emotional contact with men.

Before marriage to Bill, Kay had gone from one relationship to another. She was very sexually active yet did not enjoy sex that much. When a woman has been a surrogate spouse to her father, she will often be attracted to men like her dad but rarely enjoy the sex. Because the relationship is a re-creation of her childhood enmeshment, she will tend to give sex just to get love. On an unconscious level, the sexual aspect of the relationship feels too much like incest to be fully enjoyed. The surrogate role of the past prevented her from embracing the pleasure and vibrancy that sex offers. Through counseling, she resolved her family past and worked toward creating new patterns of love, both sexual and emotional.

A Surrogate Parent

A child can also be a surrogate parent. A surrogate parental role is one in which the child takes more responsibility for the emotional or physical well-being of the parent than the parent does for himself or herself or the child. A surrogate or substitute parental role, like a surrogate spousal one, is unhealthy for the child. It puts the parent's needs above the child's, and the child suffers. This role is frequently seen in families of alcoholics, families with a disabled parent, or families in which one or both of the parents are disengaged. The child will take on the responsibility to feel for and care for the parent even if the parent doesn't fully return the caring or closeness.

That was Betsy Breyer's story. Betsy was a competent, first-rate wife and mother; yet she had been victimized a second time by a husband who couldn't hold on to a job and then left her for another woman. In our counseling sessions we explored how her family past may have influenced the present.

Betsy talked about her dad first: "I always worried about Dad. After he and Mom divorced, he didn't take good care of himself. In between classes, I ran over to his apartment, cleaned it up, or put something in the oven for dinner. I always worried about him because Mom was so mean to him. I can still see the hurt in his eyes when she criticized him."

Betsy never closely bonded to her critical mother, and she felt sorry for her dad. He took a great deal from her but gave very little in return. Her offense and distance from Mom, coupled with a need for emotional closeness, led her to adopt a role of caretaker to her dad. Dad welcomed someone who would reach out to care for him. As someone who came from a disengaged background, he could safely find comfort in his daughter's attentiveness and in his alcohol.

A child like Betsy who has been a surrogate parent is set up for failure in her future relationships. Betsy has never learned appropriate personal boundaries—how to care for herself and others in a balanced way. She is attracted to men who appreciate and need her unbalanced caretaking because they have failed to learn how to care for themselves.

Speaking about her second marriage, Betsy lamented, "I don't know what went wrong. I did everything I could to please him. I fixed his meals, washed his clothes, and kept his house. I desperately tried to make the marriage work. I even worked overtime to keep the financial pressures off him. I just don't understand why he would leave me."

The pain of her second husband's betrayal was compounded by the repeat of the pattern. He abandoned her. Her first husband had also been a drinker who left her six months into the marriage. Betsy responded to the rejection by drawing comfort from her twelve-year-old daughter Colleen. The two of them had always been inseparable. Betsy was reenacting the unhealthy pattern of surrogacy with her daughter.

Individuals like Betsy who have to take all the responsibility for their relationships, finances, or parenting have learned unhealthy patterns of caretaking. A surrogate parental role is the major contributor to these unhealthy caretaking patterns. The more powerful the role of caretaking when a child, the greater will be the tendency to overfunction in relationships when an adult. If the pattern is not challenged and changed, it will be passed on.

The Next Generation

Children from surrogate spousal or parental backgrounds usually adopt unhealthy relationship patterns when they are grown. The most common one is to give, care, or love others too much in order to get the love so desperately needed. The excessive caretaking of their spouses and others is the result of wrongly learned personal boundaries. They have not recognized that other people must take ownership for themselves.

They carry not only their own needs but also the impossible load of meeting the needs of three or four others.

They will live out this hurtful legacy in marriage, passing on its results to the next generation by marrying a partner who needs the extra effort they offer and will continue to take without giving in return. Often people like Betsy enter into such marriages realizing that they give more than they get but believing they can get the partner to change. When they find that none of their needs are being met and their efforts to change the other person aren't working, they become deeply frustrated. The lack of emotional intimacy and sharing in the marriage encourages the unfulfilled spouse to turn to the child for need fulfillment. The chosen child becomes a surrogate, thus repeating the self-defeating cycle. If the couple divorce and don't seek healing of their unhealthy patterns, they will be prone to marry similar individuals and again perpetuate the generational pattern.

From Bad News to Good News

"What do I do now that I know everything I've done wrong?" Betsy Breyer tearfully asked. The answer to her question can be outlined by using the acronym *HOPE:*

- *Honestly* evaluate your current patterns of closeness. If a child is too close and fulfilling a surrogacy role in your life, *gradually* distance yourself. The key is to slowly provide a measure of distance in the relationship by not seeking closeness, comfort, or intimate communication as frequently. Abruptly distanced or cut off from the rich closeness that is enjoyed, a child will feel rejection. A gradual, planned withdrawal is the wisest strategy. Betsy, with the help of counseling and a close friend, gradually withdrew from Colleen. She cried less in front of Colleen and instead tried to make sure Colleen was receiving the support she needed to weather the loss of another father.

- *Openly admit and take ownership of your contribution and continuance of the problem.* The open admission of your partnering to your spouse, friends, or trusted others will keep you accountable and help you break the pattern. A word of caution: do not tell your child that you have been too close or that you need your child to tell you when you are repeating your pattern of surrogacy. This puts the responsibility on the child to monitor the adult's behavior and repeats the unhealthy surrogate pattern. Betsy asked her closest friend to help her with accountability. On a weekly basis Betsy and her friend would discuss how the week went and how Betsy had managed her relationship with Colleen. The conversations gave Betsy perspective and support.

- *Place your hope for change in God's hands by mourning your pain before Him, forgiving your past, and asking His forgiveness for yourself.* Betsy stepped back into her past and reevaluated her childhood. She revised the dreams of closeness and the patterns of love she had experienced. What she had known was what she valued and needed to change. Revisiting her past, with God's assistance, she was able to heal her love hunger and wounds of rejection. She remained in counseling for a number of months and also joined a women's support group. The group provided her with a safe place to process her past, pray, and plan for the future.

- *Educate* yourself in how to parent without partnering. Betsy needed to learn new skills of parenting. She needed exposure to new information that could help her develop new patterns of parenting that would be healthy. Merely stopping a behavior does not guarantee positive results. You must also "put on" what works, and that usually requires education. (In the next chapter, we will explore how to parent without partnering.)

It is never too late to change. These patterns of partnering are common to single-parent and blended families. The conflicts and weaknesses of the family past provoke these patterns of response. Susan and I have had to evaluate our legacies of surrogacy and set our hearts on change. In the early years of our marriage I partnered with our oldest daughter. I needed to challenge and change the pattern of surrogacy. Once Susan and I recognized the pattern, we took many of the same steps I have outlined here. The patterns changed, and our family has registered the positive result.

As described, the process of family re-creation must address the patterns and skills of parenting. In the next two chapters, I will further explore healthy and unhealthy parenting patterns. I will also explain how you can improve your parenting skills to create healthy patterns of love that can survive the test of time.

CHAPTER 9

How to Parent
Without
Partnering

How many hopes and fears, how many
ardent wishes and anxious apprehensions are
twisted together in the threads that connect
the parent with the child.

—S. G. Goodrich

René McPherson was a determined and ambitious
woman heading up a small advertising agency. Her crisp good
looks conveyed the image of a polished professional woman;
yet beneath her confident veneer, I sensed vulnerability and
loneliness. Clearing time in her busy schedule, she made an
appointment to see me because she was concerned about her
son, Bryan.

"I don't know what to do. Another counselor helped me
to see that I was overly involved with my son, so I asked him
to give me some how-tos for change. But the only thing he
told me was to stop sharing my heart with him. I've stopped

doing that, but I don't know what else to do. Can you help?'' she asked.

A divorcee, René was raising an eight-year-old son alone. From the other counselor, she found that she had unwittingly placed him in a surrogate spousal role. She shared too many of her intimate concerns with him and met too many of her needs through their relationship. She was confronted with the problem of overcoming the unhealthy pattern. She wanted a specific list of how-tos she could use, but she didn't want to take full responsibility for the needed change. Like many parents sensitized to the reality of enmeshment, she worried about hurting her son's feelings if she should withdraw some of their shared closeness.

"Who will be there for him if I'm not?" René questioned. "His father has never been loving or close. Won't Bryan see this as another parent abandoning him? And what about our friendship? Aren't we supposed to be friends? Don't all the books say you're supposed to be your child's best friend?"

Her questions reflected valid concern over her son's response to the anticipated change, but more important, they were expressions of her deep pain and fear. Enmeshment between parent and child is based not only on the parent protecting the child from emotional hurt but also on the parent receiving nurture and support from the child. René had tried to make it up to Bryan for his father's abandonment and rejection.

Bryan's dad, Joe Palermo, was an uninvolved and critical father. René cried when she told me about a tongue-lashing incident that occurred right before the divorce. Joe screamed insults at his son for misplacing one of his tools. Bryan was so traumatized by the hateful barrage that he stood in the middle of the room and wet his pants. René vowed never to let that happen to Bryan again. She was going to protect him from experiencing such humiliation again.

Parental enmeshment and surrogate relationships have a powerful component of protectionism. The parent is emotionally protecting the child's feelings or the child is caring for the parent or both. The parenting style of an enmeshed parent is characterized by overconcern about the child's emotional well-being. Many times this style is due to the absence, neglect, or authoritarian style of the other parent. The need to protect encourages partnering instead of parenting.

To overcome a surrogate role with your child, you must first understand your style of parenting. Unhealthy parenting styles are prompted by inner fears and motivations that encourage unhealthy enmeshment. Once these motivations and resulting styles are identified and resolved, you can implement workable strategies for change. The following list can assist you in identifying whether or not you are in an enmeshed relationship with your child:

- Do you have difficulty saying no to your child for fear of disappointing him or making him angry?

- Do you worry about your child a lot, going out of your way often to help her or keep her from failing?

- Do you do things for your child that he could or should be doing for himself (for example, chores, homework, personal grooming, arrangements for activities, errands, etc.)?

- Has your spouse or someone else commented to you that you do too much for your child?

- Do you have difficulty giving your child consequences for wrong behavior and sticking by them?

- Is your child the main source of pleasure and fulfillment in your life? Is your child your best friend?

- Do you feel closer to your child than to adults in your life? Do you share more easily with your child than with others? Is your child the one who seems to always comfort you when you are down or discouraged?

If you answered yes to two or more of the questions, you need to face the reality of being too close to your child.

Parenting Styles

The manner in which the parent sets rules, enforces consequences, and nurtures and communicates with the child forms a style of parenting. Family therapists have analyzed and categorized styles of parenting into four basic types that fit the vast majority of parents: (1) neglectful parents, (2) authoritarian parents, (3) permissive parents, and (4) balanced parents. Let's examine each parenting style.

Neglectful parents are not involved with the children. They may be absent from the home, or when they *are* home, they are not actively involved with children's needs for discipline and direction. Fathers may become neglectful parents due to the pressures of their work, the amount of time they must be away from home, and the resulting unfamiliarity with home routines and children's needs.

As one typical father told me, "It's too hard to work all day at the office and then switch gears when you get home, becoming a loving, attentive parent. It's much easier to let my wife do it. After all, she knows the kids and understands them much better than I do.''

Neglectful parents are frequently overwhelmed with the demands made on their lives. They are so preoccupied with other concerns, they are unable to provide the emotional support and behavioral control that children require. This frequently happens in single-parent homes and ones in which there is a lot of stress.

Parents with emotional problems, such as depression, may develop a neglectful style of parenting due to absorption in their personal problems. High-conflict marriages may produce this unhealthy preoccupation with self at the expense of the kids.

Authoritarian parents have a high need to control their children's behavior, even at the expense of the children's feelings. Authoritarian parents are primarily concerned with how the children behave.

Bryan's dad, Joe Palermo, who had been raised by a strongly authoritarian father, was repeating the pattern with Bryan: "I don't care what he thinks or how he feels. When I tell him to do something, he better do it and not give me any lip. His mother lets him get away with murder, but I expect him to behave and he knows it!"

Joe's style was similar to that of his father. When his dad told Joe to do something, Joe did it, or he would find himself laid out on the floor. Joe has hit Bryan only on rare occasions, but his attitude is still very much like his father's. He is also very angry with his ex-wife because he thinks she is too lax and doesn't make Bryan work or follow the rules. When a friend asked him about his thoughts on today's young people, Joe responded by saying, "They're all spoiled rotten. My dad made me work for what I got. These kids have it easy. They don't know what real work is."

Authoritarian parents often come from a background like Joe Palermo's where the parents demanded high performance and near-perfect behavior. Although many of the rules authoritarian parents establish are basically good ones, their lack of emotional support will convey a message not of caring but of harshness. Children will learn to think that rules count more than they do. When rules are enforced without love, they may produce outward compliance, but rebellion rages within the children. As a retired schoolteacher once said, "This kind of child will be sitting down on the outside because you told him to, but he will still be standing up on the inside."

Authoritarian parents have difficulty receiving feedback about their parenting style because they think the feedback is telling them that their rules are wrong rather than that their rules are not balanced with enough love and concern for children's emotional needs.

Permissive parents are emotionally caring, but they are overly concerned about wounding children or depriving them of inner fulfillment. These parents place a low priority on controlling children's behavior and a high priority on taking care of their feelings. Emotional protectionism is the root motivation of most enmeshed relationships, and surrogate spousal relationships often develop between permissive parents and their children.

Like René McPherson, the parent will sacrifice behavioral control to soothe the child's feelings or have the child attend to the parent's needs. The result will be a child like Bryan whose feelings have always been affirmed but who has problems with boundaries and obedient behavior.

"It's hard to get Bryan to do chores until I get really angry about it," René explained. "He plays me by pushing me to my limits. Sometimes I explode, but then I feel horribly guilty and need to make it all up to him. Usually, it's just easier for me to do things for him rather than to get him to do them for himself. I don't think he respects me like he should. He thinks he can get away with murder because I love him so much."

Permissive parents don't enforce rules and consequences because they fear crossing their children's wills. They don't want to hurt the children, and they also fear the children's anger and rejection. René worried that Bryan wouldn't love her if she set rules and required his obedience to them. The danger of permissive parenting is that children will feel loved but will not have the internal strength to do what is right when faced with the multitude of temptations this world offers. They will not have the inner discipline to say no, and they will suffer the results. They will also have difficulty sticking it out when the going gets rough and life is unfair. They will expect others to cater to their emotional needs, and they will expect not to be required to complete demanding or frustrating tasks. By being too supportive and loving, permissive parents can wound the children, making them weaker rather than stronger.

Joe Palermo's authoritarian father required him to obey, no matter how he felt. The requirement to follow the rules produced character in Joe, an inner strength or ability to do what was right, no matter how he felt. Joe's father, however, carried his demands for obedience too far, and Joe repeated the same mistake with Bryan. René, on the other hand, was too permissive with Bryan, who never learned to stick it out and do what's right, regardless of his feelings. Both need the combination that a balanced style of parenting brings.

The Best of Both Worlds

Balanced parents incorporate the need to control children's behavior with the need to support and love the children. Balanced parents have rules and requirements but enforce them with love and sensitivity to the needs of the children at the time. Anger like Joe's is not present in a balanced parenting style; but neither is René's indulgence. A balanced style administers consequences consistently and fairly in what is often called a matter-of-fact style of communication.

When Bryan didn't want to pick up his room, saying he was too tired to do it, René's parenting style would be to let him off the hook and do it for him. If Bryan used the same excuse, Joe would tell him, "I don't care how tired you are. Get yourself in gear and clean it up *now!*"

Balanced parenting coupled with a matter-of-fact communication style would offer a response like this: "Honey, I know you're tired and don't want to clean your room. I've felt that way a lot of times. But we all have to do things even when we're tired. Because you're tired, I'll give you fifteen extra minutes to do it. If you don't do your room by then, you won't be able to watch TV today."

Notice the key components in this response:

- The child's feelings of tiredness were affirmed from the beginning. That tells the child you have heard him and understand how he feels. It is important to a child to feel heard even if you do not agree with what the child wants to do as a result of the feelings.

- Saying, "We all have to do things even when we're tired," is an important part of the transaction. It teaches the child an essential rule of life. Such rules of life should be stated in universal terms, using "we" instead of "you." This makes it a rule that truly applies to everyone rather than an arbitrary one that the child feels counts only for him.

- Giving the child the extra fifteen minutes in this instance shows that you care enough to make allowances for the feelings. This is not always necessary but should be done occasionally, when appropriate. If you make allowances half or more of the time, you are being overly sensitive to his feelings and not concerned enough about his character. Allowances should be an exception, not the rule.

- "If you don't do your room by then, you won't be able to watch TV today." Stating the rule and a consequence is still the healthy order of business when dealing with a child. Even though you may be concerned about the child's tiredness, there is a need for the child to do the work and therefore suffer a consequence if he doesn't. Withdrawal of privileges is a common and helpful type of consequence compared to being on the receiving end of an angry or demanding parent.

The Parental Paradox

The sensitivity of the permissive parent and the attention to appropriate behavior of the authoritarian parent are a healthy combination for the child. Paradoxically, most parents don't use this combination. One will be permissive while the other is authoritarian. The permissive parent complains that the other is too harsh, abusive, or uncaring. The authoritarian believes that the permissive parent is too lax and protective. Many marriages come with one of each kind of parent. Both are right and wrong. What is needed is a realistic appraisal of strengths of each type of approach combined with a healthy collaboration of effort between both parents. What usually happens instead is that the battle over parenting causes an overemphasis by each parent on respective areas of weakness.

"The harsher Joe was with Bryan, the more I felt the need to protect him," René reflected. "I'm sure that Joe saw my protection as a challenge to his authority. Each of us got more entrenched in the belief that the other person was wrong. I now see how it had become a vicious cycle, with both of us feeding its power and Bryan suffering the result."

A big first step toward change is the *recognition* of parenting style coupled with an understanding of how it influences the partner's parenting efforts. René was able to see how she and Joe had contributed to each other's negative parenting style. I encouraged René to meet with Joe and discuss with him what she had learned about herself and their respective styles. Both parents' recognition of the strengths and weaknesses of their styles can yield positive results. Additionally, their realizations can help to take the power struggle out of parenting.

"Thank you for calling this meeting," Joe declared. "I was hesitant to come because I thought it would result in another fight where you insist that you're right and I'm wrong. It looks like we're both wrong and need to do something about it. I'm up to changing if you are."

Joe was relieved to hear that he was not the culprit. René's willingness to admit her error paved the way for Joe to let down his resistance and cooperate with her on Bryan's behalf. The "I'm right and you're wrong" attitude is a reflection of that person's need to be affirmed for positive contributions. When one parent can affirm the strength of the other's style, change and collaboration become much easier. However, to fully conquer the unhealthy styles and become balanced in parenting, individuals may also need to step back into the past.

Another major step toward change lies in the discovery of influences from the past that helped create our parenting styles with our own children. Uncovering these hidden influences and motivations helps us break their power and embrace a new style.

The Motivating Roots

Our parenting styles develop first from the styles of our parents. Few of us ever take a course in parenting; rather, we learn by what we lived with growing up. Joe learned how to discipline from his father with an angry and authoritarian style. René's style was a mirror image of her father's. René experienced difficulty in her relationship with her mom, who was a critical and demanding person. She bonded more closely with her father, who was more sympathetic and concerned about her feelings. Her dad was permissive and her mom authoritarian. Though grown up now, she still smarted from the biting tongue-lashings of her childhood. The feeling prompted her to respond to Bryan as her father had cared for her. It also caused her to believe, "I need to be there for Bryan. My mom wasn't there for me and it hurt. I need to protect him from his dad like my dad protected me."

When we are wounded in childhood by the neglect, abuse, or harshness of a parent, we make inner judgments and vows about what has happened. These inner evaluations and self-promises form attitudes and beliefs that guide our future responses. Joe's inner evaluation of his dad's abusiveness was that he, Joe, was deficient and needed to do whatever his dad demanded. Joe vowed never to let his dad's anger hurt him;

he was going to be man enough to take it. His defense against the inner pain was to toughen up and deny that it hurt. This caused him to mimic his dad's harsh and abusive style of discipline. Joe's motto was, "If it was good enough for me, it's good enough for Bryan."

In contrast to Joe, René's hurtful relationship with her mom and her supportive one with her dad encouraged her to adopt the following beliefs:

- "If I don't protect Bryan, he'll think that I don't love him."

- "Caring about his feelings is the most important thing I can do to show him I love him."

- "I need to be there for him at all times. I need to be his best friend."

Although it is true that individuals need protection during childhood and that part of love is protection, it is not true that we should protect children from all hurt and that a lack of full protection is a lack of love. Love, by definition, seeks the best for the object of love. It is not in the best interest of children to protect them from every hurt. If this is done, children grow up with emotional disabilities, unable to fully face and resolve the hurts that come as part of the natural process of life.

The opposite extreme is also harmful. The harshness and demands of authoritarian parents will wound the inner being of children, causing anger, defensiveness, and insensitivity. Children raised by authoritarian parents will have difficulty with intimacy and closeness. The inner part of the person is too protected to enter into the emotional sharing and vulnerability that intimacy requires.

A child raised by a permissive parent will often unconsciously use rejection of the parent as a blackmail device to get his way. Bryan was able to manipulate René into doing what he wanted by pouting and feigning rejection of her. Immediately, René would give in to his demands because she did not want to risk his rejection. Her belief that Bryan would not love her if she didn't caretake his feelings became a self-protective device to keep him from hurting her feelings. In reality, *her* sensitivity to rejection was the motivating factor behind her actions, and her love for Bryan was in part a manipulation to assure that he would love her. She was giving love to get it back, afraid to discipline him—fearing he would withdraw his love from her if she did.

Being constantly vigilant to not hurt someone's feelings is not the most important thing one person can do for another. Caring about how someone feels is important, but so are the building of character and the inculcating of values that transcend feelings. Bryan was already establishing a reputation of poor self-discipline and manipulative behavior in school. René did not teach him how to apply internal controls on his impulses and emotions. Character development helps a child be successful. It helps a child learn personal discipline and self-control.

A third belief of René's that is common to most enmeshed parents is that they need to be the child's best friend. The child doesn't need the parent to always be a best friend. The child needs to establish friendships with peers as well as parents. A basic part of a child's socialization process is making and maintaining friendships. When the parent is the child's constant confidant and companion, the child will lack age-appropriate social skills.

Friendship is most appropriate as an adolescent approaches the age of maturity. At this time the parent should make a transition from being an authority in the child's life toward being a friend. This is the time when the development of a more collaborative relationship is warranted. An enmeshed parent has a hard time letting go of the closeness while an authoritarian parent rarely is close and therefore doesn't develop a friendship with the child. Both types of parents need to examine child-parent relationships and adjust accordingly.

Resolving the Roots

René needed healing for her past before she could appropriately parent her son. The unresolved wounds from her childhood were the motivating forces behind her need to partner and protect Bryan. When Bryan hurt, René felt for him in great part because of her pain. His hurt subconsciously triggered her unresolved wound from the past and made her protective response much stronger than necessary.

Joe also needed healing from his past. For him, the healing began when he was able to admit to himself how much his father's harshness had wounded him. Joe's counterdependent style of relationship prized invulnerability and toughness. Those attitudes made him resistant to counseling. René's change of attitude encouraged him to pursue counseling with me. It helped Joe uncover the unhealthy roots of his family past and begin the journey to wholeness.

Both disengaged and enmeshed parents respond to their children out of the unresolved pain of their childhoods or marriages. The enmeshed ones have become sensitized to emotional wounding to such a degree they can't stand to see someone they love also hurt. The disengaged ones have become insensitive to the pain of others or themselves. Healing for both requires revisiting the wounds of the past and gaining full resolution.

Prayer is an essential part of healing. It is a personal recognition of the need coupled with an invitation to God, asking for His healing touch and empowering love.

If reading this chapter has made you aware of ways in which you have partnered a child or been wounded by your parents, the following prayer may help:

Dear heavenly Father,

I am grieved over how I may have wounded _____ *(name of child)* because of my unhealthy parenting. I ask You to forgive me. Give me the wisdom and the power to change. I also pray for my child and ask You to reverse the course of my imperfect parenting. Take what has been wrong and turn it for good in _____'s life as only You can.

Last, I ask You to heal my heart. My _____ *(Mom, Dad, etc.)* didn't parent me right. Her/His/Their weaknesses have wounded me, causing me to hurt the ones I love. Help me to forgive her/him/them for the deficiencies. Break these generational strongholds of unbalanced parenting. Amen.

In the following chapter, we will explore the dynamics of parenting in blended families. These families encounter additional challenges as they try to create healthy legacies of love.

CHAPTER 10

The
Equation
Family

*Multimarriages have spawned another
dimension: equation families. A whole
brother and two half-sisters divided by two
mothers (one step) equals a whole father plus
a weekend dad divided by seven grandparents
(subtract two who have died), including two
others who have married and multiplied.*

—Erma Bombeck

Erma Bombeck's humorous description of equation families is not far from the truth. Single-parent and blended families have proliferated in the past ten to fifteen years. In the 1950s, seven out of ten homes in America were made up of traditional families, those composed of partners in a first marriage and their biological children. Recent statistics indicate that the percentages have reversed. Only three out of ten homes are comprised of traditional families; the rest are made up of blended families, single-parent families, childless couples, and singles. This change of family structure has complicated the bonding patterns and discipline strategies each family must exercise and has raised troubling questions:

- Should a stepfather closely bond to a teenage daughter?

- Should single-parent mothers find substitute dads for their kids?

- What about teenage sons? Are they to remain close to Mom or be given free rein?

- Should a teenage son submit to the authority and discipline of a new stepfather? If so, to what degree?

These are but a few of the many questions that changes in family structure have raised. Change is always stressful. With the added pressures and confusion of divorce, single parenting, and remarriage, unhealthy relationships and parenting patterns have increased. Divorce, single parenting, and remarriage are powerful shapers of relationship. They particularly affect children. They can cause pain and difficulty for generations through the bonding relationships they alter and the negative patterns they can encourage.

For example, the pain of divorce can be so great that it results in neglect of the children. Mom and Dad are too preoccupied with their own struggles to care for the needs of the children, thus encouraging distance and disengagement in the children. A disengaged dad, when divorced, becomes even more distant and disengaged from his children. Enmeshment, short-term or long-term, is also a danger. A parent who is already close to a child may draw too close to receive comfort from the pain of marital separation. A mother who was close to her child may wound the child when she remarries by giving the love and attention the child was receiving to the new spouse. Even if the mother has been enmeshed with her child and is making a healthy transition, the result can be wounding to the child.

Changes in family structure provoke other weaknesses as well. René McPherson shared how her attitudes and life changed when she divorced Bryan's dad: "I became touchy and irritable. I was so hurt by Bryan's dad that I walked around angry all the time. Even though I drew Bryan closer to me, I also was more impatient and critical of him. Then I felt so guilty over my reactions to Bryan that I bought him anything he wanted to make it up to him." The emotional stress of her divorce fueled René's enmeshment with Bryan and encouraged a permissive style of parenting.

Sharon Ramsey, a friend of René's, also had divorced her husband. She met René in a singles group at church, and the two became friends. Her reaction to the dissolution of her marriage, however, was different from René's. She became more disengaged and neglectful of her two boys.

"When I divorced Jim, I didn't care anymore. I went out drinking and partying every chance I got. He had been unfaithful to me, and I wasn't about to stay home and take it. What I didn't realize is how much my absence hurt the boys. I left them at my mom's house all the time. I also left them at home with each other a lot. That's when they got into fighting with each other," she said.

Changes in the stability of the marriage encourage mismanagement of the children. Pain stimulates personal strongholds. Previously stable individuals can become bitter, fearful, distraught, or even abusive. Faithful marriage partners may become promiscuous or problem drinkers. Each of these responses will affect the children in negative ways.

For Sharon Ramsey, a change in marital status developed into a neglectful style of parenting. The marital pain put her needs in conflict with the children's, and they lost. Divorce, single parenting, and even remarriage create a conflict between the needs of the children for healthy love, care, and discipline and the needs of the parent.

Sharon's older son, Billy, told me what happened when she divorced his dad: "My mom was gone a lot, and we had to stay at Grandma's house. It was boring, and there wasn't anyone to play with. My brother, Jerry, and I fought a lot."

Eleven-year-old Billy also shared some of the feelings he experienced when Mom was gone all night. "I was worried about her. I didn't want her to leave like Dad did. I tried to take care of Jerry, but he wouldn't do anything I told him to. He just sat in front of the TV."

Billy's worry is common to most kids who experience the trauma of their parents' divorce, as are guilt and even anger. Children may think they are responsible for the breakup. They may be angry with either or both parents for the loss of their family or the hurtful way a parent behaves. Children, however, do not easily communicate their feelings and thoughts to parents. More often they express themselves through changes in behavior. They become quieter than usual or more agitated. They may do poorly at school and spend more time away from the house with their friends or even by themselves. They are moody. Simple requests from a parent may provoke surly replies.

Children may go to the opposite extreme, becoming overly compliant, solicitous, and even parental in attitude. Hurting, troubled, or disengaged parents can provoke caretaking roles in their children. They want to make up for the loss, feeling a responsibility to care for the parent's or sibling's feelings. Sharon's absence intensified Billy's worry and his need to protect and parent his brother. Billy wanted to take care of them both. The fights with his brother started when Billy tried to parent Jerry, and Jerry resisted his parenting.

Beneath these symptoms is a wounded heart crying out for healing, understanding, and love. A rebellious teenager may respond to inner hurt by reacting angrily and defiantly. A withdrawn child responds to the same hurt in a different way. Parents need to encourage more healthy behavior and help heal their children's inner wounds. If children do not resolve the hurts of parents' broken marriage, as adults they will react out of this wound, adopting unhealthy patterns of relationship in an attempt to get and give the love they need. These patterns may be further exacerbated if children are required to accept a new father, brother, or sister. Rather than healing the wounds, the new family creates more. These unhealed wounds of love hunger from childhood empower the unhealthy patterns of adulthood and in turn pass on the enmeshed or disengaged legacy of pain to future generations.

What's a Parent to Do?

The key for change in a child or an adolescent lies with the parents. Even though an adolescent may be engaging in totally unacceptable behavior, parents must first deal with their contribution to the adolescent's problem. Parents have more power and God-given authority for change than does a child or an adolescent. When parents first take responsibility for their actions, they are modeling for the child the healthy lesson of taking responsibility for one's behavior. This lesson must be embraced by a child or an adolescent before healing and healthy living can commence. Too often we parents require our children to change without taking our share of responsibility. "Do what I say, not what I do" is not an effective slogan for raising children. Numerous studies have shown that modeling is the most effective teacher.

Does this mean that parents are to blame for all of their children's problems? Absolutely not. Every child has a free will, and the older the child, the more responsibility the child should take for behavior. It is still true, however, that family life in general and parents in particular are the major shapers of a child's character. When parents take responsibility for a problem first, they help to rectify what they may have done to contribute to the problem—as if they are removing logs from a burning fire. They may have unwittingly fueled the fire of rebellion, depression, or whatever by adding logs to the child's pile. The child lit the match by making a decision to head in a certain direction or behave in a specific manner. When confronted with the child's problem behavior, parents may have added gasoline instead of water to the fire by reacting to the problem in a wrong or hurtful manner.

Taking responsibility is an open recognition of the logs one has contributed to the fire (problem) as well as the way one has reacted once the fire has become apparent. Taking responsibility by recognizing one's contribution, however, does not release the child from assuming her responsibility for the decisions she's made and the course she's taken.

Ten Steps to Responsibility

"What should I do?" Sharon asked. "Should I tell Jerry and Billy that I was wrong in leaving them with my mother so much or what? Do I have to confess to them how much I drank and slept around?"

Taking responsibility for one's actions should begin first with God, not with others. As Sharon realizes how she has wounded her children, she must make amends, beginning with God. She should then seek counsel from others as to how to proceed with the children. An unwarranted or wrongly managed confession can cause a child as much pain as a neglectful season of parenting. A good rule of thumb to follow is this: the younger the child, the less explanation is needed. Both Billy and Jerry were old enough that Sharon could make direct amends to them. The following would be a partial list of tasks she must accomplish with each child:

1. Sharon needs to admit she left them with her mother too much, asking their forgiveness and explaining that it was not their fault.

2. She needs to quiet the fears of abandonment by telling each one that she will not leave him and then follow through on her promise by modeling consistent care, concern, and a stable home life.

3. She must encourage both children to realize that the divorce was not their fault. (Children commonly feel responsible for the loss of a parent, thinking they weren't good enough and somehow caused the breakup of the marriage.)

4. She must not blame or criticize her husband to them or in front of them. Young children and early age adolescents are not mature enough to understand the obvious and not-so-obvious causes of divorce. Besides, a description by one spouse is rarely the whole truth. Simple answers that are truthful, but avoid blame, are the best policy.

5. She must ask forgiveness for the divorce. Neither child caused or wanted the divorce. Sharon and her husband had the responsibility to provide a stable and enduring family life for the children. Her willingness to take responsibility for her failure acknowledges the impact the marital split had on the boys. If she did not want the divorce and did everything possible to resolve the conflict, her apology will be one of identifying with their loss more than accepting blame.

6. She must grieve the dissolution of the marriage and allow her sons to do so as well. The breakup of even the most painful marriage, though accompanied by some sense of relief, is also the shattering of hopes and dreams. A period of expressed mourning over the loss is appropriate and healthy.

7. Sharon must establish healthy bonding patterns with her boys. Both need her to be closely connected to them but not so closely that it interferes with healthy individuation. She needs to make sure that they are not *her* confidants but that she is theirs. She must also provide discipline and direction for the boys' lives. Her neglectful style of discipline must be changed to a balanced one.

8. She should explore healthy ways for the children to remain in relationship with their father. The boys need a father's input and closeness in their lives. She must not encourage their disengagement from their dad or his from them unless, of course, there is a serious problem of abuse. Even in such a case the sons need to speak respectfully, yet honestly, about their father.

9. Whatever lingering feelings of bitterness or resentment exist, Sharon must overcome them for her benefit and for the children's. Healthy communication must be established between her and her ex-husband for the sake of the children. *Partners* may divorce each other, but *parents* never do. Both retain the responsibility to parent their children until adulthood. Wherever possible, collaboration of effort and unity of direction in parenting must prevail.

10. If Sharon remarries, she must clarify, prior to marriage, the expectations of relationship and discipline the stepdad will have with the boys. This negotiation should include the biological dad. The collaboration of all three ensures that unhealthy patterns do not develop and that the desired unity of purpose and style of discipline is maintained.

    If remarried, Sharon must actively work toward inviting and including her new husband into the family system. Shared activities and healthy "I care" messages (see Chapter 2) that encourage bonding must be a high priority. The process of bonding and inclusion of the stepfather into the family will have its own unique pattern and timetable. If, however, the bonding or relationship patterns are not working well, Sharon and the family would need to seek counseling. For blended families, the road-blocks to healthy love are usually rooted in the trauma of the past.

This is a general game plan. Obviously, variations exist. But such steps are essential to the maintenance or creation of a stable home and family life for the children. The negative patterns of getting and giving love often arise from the un-healed wounds of divorce.

Parenting Wounds

The hurtful ways parents like Sharon Ramsey affect their children's lives are called *parenting wounds*. Divorce, abuse, ne-glect, and both disengaged and enmeshed parenting styles can cause wounds in children. Parents can also be overly critical, impatient, or indulgent. Each attitude registers its effects on children and influences their eventual choice of parenting styles. When children become adults, they may try to re-create what they never had from their parents, or they may follow their parents' example exactly, repeating their mis-takes.

In reconstituted or stepfamilies, parenting wounds can be especially severe. This is true for several reasons:

- Children are already in an emotionally vulnerable state due to the trauma of the divorce. When their custodial parent decides to remarry, they are suddenly forced to relate intimately to a new parent and perhaps new step-brothers and stepsisters. Such radical changes evoke their fears of abandonment and rejection, and make any wounds they receive especially painful.

- Parents experience increased stress as they struggle to adapt to each other and a new marriage. The addition of children to the "instant family" system makes the adjustment much more complex. Divided loyalties, miscommunication, and differences in parenting style often place biological parents in the crossfire between children and stepparents.

- Stepfamilies experience a lengthy period of confusion about the role of each individual. Role confusion increases tension and conflict, a fertile ground for inflicting parental wounds.

Whether you were raised in a traditional, single-parent, or stepfamily setting, you must recognize the parenting wounds of your childhood. People frequently ignore their parenting wounds and their impact on shaping who they are and how they parent. Responsible parenting requires discovering how the wounds affected you then and how they influence you now in your relationships with your children.

The following discussion describes the most common parenting wounds. Thoughtfully examine how your parents and/or caretakers related to you. If you were raised in a reconstituted or stepfamily, think about your relationships with your biological parents and your stepparent. Also consider how your parents' style of parenting affected you and your parenting today.

For example, if you were raised in a home with a perfectionistic, rigid, or controlling parent, you may rarely feel good about yourself. You may feel you never measure up to your parent's standards. Mistakes were not tolerated or easily forgiven, making it hard for you now, as an adult, to accept the mistakes you make and forgive yourself for them. Both permissive and authoritarian parents can develop from this background. Permissive parents vow never to be as rigid, controlling, or perfectionistic as their parent was. This vow leads them to overcompensate, becoming too loose with the rules and too flexible with the consequences for wrongdoing. Authoritarian parents, on the other hand, feel that they should have met each one of their parent's demands. They become controlling and demanding.

When children are raised in a home with a lot of anger, abuse, or punishment, they can become fearful or angry. Fearful children are timid and compliant, thinking that they are responsible for the anger and abuse they receive. They suffer from low self-worth and one-way relationship patterns. Their tendency as adults will be to err on the side of permissive styles of parenting. Children who respond in anger to parental abuse will tend to be authoritarian as parents. They are filled with the hurt, anger, and resentment that come from the anger or abuse. When others cross their wills or fail to live up to their expectations, their anger and frustration will spill out.

If you were raised by absent, inattentive, or neglectful parents, you may feel you don't count. Neglectful parents convey the message that the child is not important enough to warrant their attention. Stepparents, especially fathers, often follow this pattern. Divorced, noncustodial parents can easily err in this way, also. If your parents were neglectful, you may develop either a neglectful or a permissive style of parenting. You may become a permissive parent who wants only to love and be loved by your child.

Healing the Past

Children need close, long-lasting, positive attachments with both parents until they're grown. They also need discipline, direction, and consistent consequences for wrong behavior. Functional family structures are stable ones that encourage and maintain this healthy balance of connection while limiting negative styles of discipline. The marriage must be solid to provide appropriate connection and discipline for the kids. Family structural changes through divorce, single parenting, or remarriage rip and tear at the very fabric of one's ability to give and receive love in a healthy manner. These changes can create or reinforce generational strongholds of enmeshment and disengagement, coupled with unbalanced caretaking roles. They also provoke unhealthy patterns of parental discipline.

Marriages need support and care to work well. Research indicates that most second marriages will fail if the couples do not get counseling. When the first marriage has not worked, both partners, the children, the prospective spouses, the stepchildren, and even the grandparents need healing and instruction to overcome the inherent problems and create healthy patterns. This step assures that strongholds will not be passed on through the generations.

If through divorce, single parenting, or remarriage, you have caused your children or someone else's children to suffer, it is never too late to remedy the situation. Accept the truth and responsibility of your actions first before God. Pray to Him, acknowledging your shortcomings and hurtful behavior and asking His forgiveness. This humbling of self before God is always a prerequisite to change. God resists the proud but gives grace to the humble. He will also give you wisdom on what steps to take to make things better. Cleaning up the past may also require you to take the steps outlined for Sharon Ramsey.

If you are enmeshed with your child rather than disengaged, follow the same steps, making allowances for being too close rather than too far. One word of caution: if you are too close to a child and you need to distance yourself, *don't* make amends for being too close. The child will not understand. Instead, slowly distance yourself by no longer sharing intimate adult concerns with the child, and implement a sound program of rules and consequences for any behavioral problems. These actions will resolve the enmeshment over time.

Finally, face your wounds. Change requires that you, as the parent, step back and resolve your past. There are commonly accepted methods to healing these hurtful patterns from childhood. The process requires you to reexamine the past in light of new evidence, allow the painful feelings resulting from the wounds to resurface, and then release the pain. Chapter 12 goes into detail on how to heal wounds of the past.

Each of us needs to put aside the fears, wounds, problems, and perspectives of the past. The words of the apostle Paul to the Corinthians affirm this: "When I was a child, I spoke as a child, I understood as a child, I thought as a child; but when I became a man, I put away childish things" (1 Cor. 13:11). The words, the understanding, and the thoughts of childhood are not adequate for living adult life. With God's help you can be free of the chains of childhood memories, misunderstanding, misjudgment, and love hunger.

Pray for mature wisdom and God's perspective to see your childhood clearly, forgive its hurts, and revoke its power to control you any longer. Also pray for the strength to take full responsibility for your contribution to the hurts and pains of someone else's childhood.

And practice new patterns of love and connection by adding positive "I care" messages to your existing relationships. Healthy love behaviors help to heal the rifts and pains of the past, and children respond quickly to demonstrated care and concern. Direct and indirect "I care" behaviors, practiced on a routine basis, will create healthy patterns of connection with most children. Part 5 presents exercises that help families prevent lingering wounds and offenses from interfering with the healthy love patterns as well as ones that create closeness and shared communication. Re-creating family is a changing of love patterns and also an attitude of heart that fosters truthful, yet loving communication.

RE-CREATED FAMILIES

Re-creating family bonds of love takes our willingness and God's power. As we recognize the unhealthy patterns and take ownership for our contribution, health results. New patterns are created as we reshape our family dream and share the truth in love.

CHAPTER 11

The Family
Dream

Man only has two things in life, dreams and
the courage to fulfill them.
—Rick Howard

We have examined how the family past influences us and, in turn, our families, marriages, and children. We have attempted to bring to awareness the largely unconscious shaping of our lives. We have seen how the distance of disengagement and overly close bonding of enmeshment can be hurtful. We have explored how marriage and even parenting styles can be affected by the dynamic of closeness, and we have examined how children register predictable results of unhealthy bonding patterns.

There is another component of family love that must be examined—the family dream. Deep within each one of us is a very specific picture of our ideal family. This inner vision of fulfillment is what I call the *family dream*. It holds the hopes for the future for ourselves and our children. It is a composite of what each of us wants and doesn't want in a family. The family dream is the inner construct for creating the family values, structures, and love we want.

Remember Sharon Carpenter and her family in Chapter 1? Her dream was for a family structure she never had: "The one thing I have always wanted is to give Kelly and her younger sister Jennifer a family. It's the one thing that makes me feel so guilty. I never had a family, and I know what it feels like. But look at the mess I've made. Kelly is in trouble, Philip works all the time, and I'm home alone with Jennifer. That's not the way I wanted it," Sharon protested.

For Sharon, the dream was for a family structure she never had. Raised in a single-parent home, Sharon always wanted a dad like other kids had. She vowed to never let what she experienced happen to her children. When the divorce from Ed was finalized, she became seriously depressed. Her dream of creating an ideal family for her children was shattered. Marrying Philip rekindled the hope of fulfillment but then disappointed her again. Sharon's dream pictured a family where Philip would come home early for supper and play with the kids, and she wouldn't have to work. It was one of closeness and intimate sharing. Sadly, her dream was again being thwarted. Philip worked late and had little time to develop intimacy with his new wife and daughters. Kelly was often gone, and Jennifer went her own way with her friends. Sharon was again frustrated and depressed. She needed to acknowledge and examine her family dream, understanding why it was so important to her and what she could do about it.

Where Dreams Come From

The inner visions of what we hope for are our dreams. Dreams are some of life's most powerful motivators. They are the driving forces that stir us to rise above the humdrum of daily life, seize opportunities, and express creative abilities. In every story of great or unusual human accomplishment there is an empowering dream, one that challenges the person to be more, do more, or think differently than otherwise would occur. This is the blessing of dreams. They are God's way of directing the human spirit toward accomplishment and fulfillment. They are also the impetus for making things better or different, especially when we have suffered or failed. Dreams offer the inner being new life and hope for something better.

Our past experiences, both good and bad, cause us to form an inner image or dream of what we would like family life to be for us. Because the inner being or spirit is easily wounded by the pressures, problems, and sin of this world, dreams are generally connected to our wounds. When wounded, we can become hopeless and helpless. The vision of a happy future diminishes. We retreat from risking the vulnerability that life and love require. It is easy to become hard and cynical, to not try again. But a dream, a vision of something better, offers us the hope we need to run the race for the prize of fulfillment. A dream is the hope that we can create a future that is better than the past. It is also a desire to replicate the good experiences of the past that we don't want to lose. Family dreams are the deep desires of heart and spirit that want to hold on to the good and reshape the bad.

However, few of us are consciously aware of the family dream and how it was formed. Sharon Carpenter's dream in great part came from her family past and the love hunger it created. She was attempting to redo her past and make up for her hunger for a dad's love by assuring her children never lacked that love. Her dream of family came from the missing elements of her childhood.

Philip Carpenter's family dream also came from a deficient childhood but one that was quite different from Sharon's. "My dad was a strict disciplinarian and hard worker," Philip stated. "He never showed much affection to us while we were growing up and always made sure we toed the line. If any of us kids got out of line, we could count on a swift beating from Dad. We respected our dad even though he didn't show much love. I swore that when I grew up, I would make sure my family respected me."

Philip's dream of family was a repeat of what he experienced as a child. He felt that his father's abusive discipline had been good for him and that he needed to do the same with his children. Sharon's kids, Kelly and Jennifer, were shocked the first time Philip laid into them. Sharon was outraged, but Philip was adamant in his defense of the value it would have for them in later years. Philip also defended his need to work long hours, saying, "My dad did it, and it's what got us through the tough times. If I don't work, who's going to provide for the family? Do you think money just grows on trees?"

Philip's dream also was created by his love hunger. Philip's way of responding to the lack of affection, care, and intimacy from his dad was to defend and emulate him. When one defends or emulates an undesirable or unhealthy trait in a parent, it is an attempt to deny the pain and consequences the trait produces. It was Philip's unhealthy way of resolving the hurt of his dad's abusive discipline and rejection.

Experiences in childhood that deprive us of the love we

need can mar the blueprint for the family dream. If our parents or caretakers fail to meet our deepest needs for love, attention, care, affection, affirmation, or acceptance, we can develop a love hunger that shapes the future family dream into a flawed one. The wounded spirit causes us to desire and hope for what was lacking or lost. The unhealed wound propels us to create what was missing, to re-create a set of circumstances and relationships that will fulfill our needs and heal our hurts. Sharon and Philip Carpenter were still responding in the present to the wounds of the past. Both must recognize and resolve the wounds their family dreams were built upon in order to change the patterns. They also must re-create the flawed family dream, fashioning it into a healthy one.

Expectations of Love

Interestingly enough, sometimes the excessive meeting of needs can create a love hunger that then compels us to want to re-create what we had. Let me give you an example from my life. Raised by an unusually attentive and supportive mother, I received abundant amounts of care, love, support, and affection. Unwittingly, I built expectations of continued excessive love into my family dream. I expected my wife, Susan, to be exactly like Mom. Because of the excessive love of my past, I felt wounded when Susan or others did not provide it again. I had come to expect it, and I felt defrauded when it was not forthcoming.

Inherent in family dreams are our expectations of how we want to be loved and the demands of others to meet those expectations. Many of us seek the love we never had, and we demand that others provide it. Our present dreams are based on hurtful past experiences rather than on what the reality of the present says is healthy. My expectations of love were unrealistic. The demands I placed on others to fulfill my dreams of love were wrong and needed to be released.

But what if our expectations are healthy and yet are not being met? We must still surrender the demand. The expectation does not have to change, but the demand for its fulfillment must. We must never demand love, care, or concern from others even when it may be rightfully due. The demand for fulfillment is symptomatic of the wound within, not just the circumstances without. Focusing on the demand keeps us from resolving the wound within. The necessity of laying down demands to resolve pain is a truth many people never understand. Sharon Carpenter came to this truth during one of our sessions.

"I know I've been too angry and demanding," Sharon confessed. "It's just that it's so hard to see everything I have worked for go down the tubes. I need companionship and love like everybody else. I wish Philip and the girls would see that. But I also realize I can't force them to love me or to make up for my past."

Sharon's recognition was a major step forward. Even though her love hunger and frustrated family dream were not resolved, she realized her anger and demands were not the answer. The family past creates the love hunger and love pattern that fuel the family dream. Within the dream emerges a set of expectations of how others should love, care, or relate. When our expectations are dashed, so are our hopes. In response, it is easy to become demanding, controlling, or reactive, always blaming others for not loving us. Like Sharon, I openly pressured and demanded. Others show their disappointment and demand through withdrawal and the cold shoulder.

It is crucial to recognize and take ownership for the unhealthy ways we react when others don't meet our needs or fulfill our dreams and expectations. If we don't take a step back and examine our reactions, we run the risk of remaining part of the problem instead of the solution. Our preoccupation with others and our unmet needs keep us from uncovering and releasing the love hunger that fuels the problem. Recognizing how we pursue the dream and how we react when it is not being realized is a step we must all take on the journey toward re-creating family.

Living Another's Dream

We may also respond to the past by adopting another person's dream and demanding its fulfillment. I saw a graphic example of this truth in Ted Whitman's family. A self-employed mechanic, Ted was raised in the Ozarks and moved west after marrying his childhood sweetheart, Dodie. Ten years into their marriage, the honeymoon was definitely over. Dodie worried about their finances and complained about Ted's lack of attentiveness to her and the children.

During one of our Family Week sessions, Dodie opened her heart to the group: "He is never home. He's always helping someone else instead of working. Last week it was the pastor of the new church we are attending. He helped them lay the carpet and move in all the furniture. But if I ask him to help me or to work more to pay our bills, he always finds a way out of it. We're almost ready to be evicted from our home, and he is still down at the church helping them. I just don't understand why."

Ted readily admitted his lack of responsiveness to Dodie and their financial problems, but he also admitted that he felt powerless to change. As we probed to discover the roots of his pattern, he reluctantly shared the following: "My dad's dream was to buy the sawmill up the road from the house and start our own timber business with my older brother and me. For years we did side jobs, trying to get enough money for the down payment. But everything went to pot when my brother died in a freak accident. Dad started drinking heavily and withdrew from all of us. He never recovered, dying the year before I moved out here. I still get choked up when I think of him and my brother."

Ted's willingness to help everyone else while not fulfilling his responsibilities was a direct result of his brother's death and the Whitman family's crushed dream. In a strange way Ted was re-creating *his* family dream by helping other men fulfill *their* dreams, just as he helped his dad and brother. He wanted to recapture the good times and feelings he experienced with them, and he craved the camaraderie and teamwork they shared. His dad always said, "I can't do this without you boys." Unwittingly, because Ted latched on to his dad's dream, he was still trying to live it out. The wound of the past was still controlling the present.

Reexamining Your Dream

When family life doesn't work the way you want it to, it can be God's way of saying that you must reexamine the dream or change the way you've followed it. To enjoy a healthy and fulfilling family life for yourself and your loved ones, you may need to fashion a new, healthier dream, one that assures you give and get love in healthy ways.

Ted needed to let go of his father's dream and find a new one, one that was realistic and fulfilling for himself, Dodie, and the kids. The Carpenters and the Whitmans needed new dreams that offered them the opportunity to get and give love. They also faced the challenge of changing the ways in which they pursued their dreams.

This need to reexamine our dreams and how we reach them is not a modern-day phenomenon. For centuries humankind has been faced with the task of fashioning and pursuing dreams. Remember our friend from the Bible, Abraham, and his family? As we look at his life, we will discover the important elements for forming and pursuing a healthy family dream.

Abraham's Dream

Abraham was childless. He and his wife, Sarah, were well up in years, and there was no heir to his vast holdings. In biblical times that was a particularly traumatic condition. Children were seen as proof of God's favor, and sons were desired in order to safely pass on the family heritage and possessions. One day in a vision God appeared to Abraham and promised him a son who would come from his own loins. Though believing in God's promise, Abraham watched the years go by, and Sarah remained barren. In frustration, Sarah approached Abraham and asked him to conceive a child through her maidservant Hagar. Foolishly, Abraham agreed and Hagar became pregnant.

But problems immediately surfaced. Hagar acted as though she was the wife instead of Sarah's servant. Sarah became enraged, and she blamed Abraham. Seeing the error of his ways, he gave Sarah permission to do whatever she desired with Hagar. Hagar, banished by Sarah, later returned and submitted to Sarah before Ishmael was born.

Ishmael became known as the child of the flesh, meaning he was conceived out of Abraham and Sarah's vain attempt to pursue their dream. He was not the child of God's promise. Abraham's attempt to fulfill the dream that he and God shared brought strife, resentment, and rejection. Though an heir was born, the result was second best. As we shall later see, the child of promise did arrive, but even then there was a challenge.

Some elements of Abraham's story are more applicable to biblical times than to our times. However, there are a number of unique aspects of his family dream that all successful dreams share. The first is that our dreams must always be ones that God values. Abraham's desire for a son was matched by God's desire to give him one. Too many of our dreams are ones that only we want. They have not been formed with God's approval.

Dreams are too important to leave to our whims. We need God's guidance and direction for our lives. Our love hungers can easily distort our vision and produce failed dreams. Biblical truth and prayer must anchor the expression of our dreams, or we will risk their failure.

Ted Whitman's dream was his, not his and God's. God has a unique destiny and dream for Ted, but he was too preoccupied with the unfulfilled family dream of his past to find out what God wants for his future.

"I prayed like you asked me to," Ted told me. "And I couldn't believe what happened. It was like a picture that someone drew on a wall. I just knew it was God talking to me. I saw how I have been looking everywhere else but to Him for the guidance I need. I wanted to help others pursue their dreams because I was afraid of forming my own goal in life. I'm still not sure what all this means, but for the first time in my life I feel like God is for me, and something good is going to happen."

Ted's attempt to include God in his dreams was already paying dividends. He was on the road to discovery and fulfillment. But a second challenge awaits him and us when we come to the point of embracing the dream that God has forged with us. The test then is how we pursue the dream. Abraham, through Sarah's pressure, attempted it on his own. The results were disastrous. How many times have we been in a similar situation, ruing the day we acted on what we thought was a good idea? For a good dream to come true, we must prayerfully submit to God the dream and the steps we take to fulfill it. Asking for His wisdom and guidance and resisting the pressure of others or of our own love hungers are our only assurances of success.

A dream is a lifelong process lived out over time. If we try to make it happen on our terms or timetable, we risk forfeiting God's partnership with us. Losing His input and assistance will doom or severely limit the dream. Tragic stories are shared daily in counseling offices across the continent of those who married or became involved with others out of their love hungers and ill-advised decisions. God will always help us achieve what He desires for our lives—but only if we cooperate with Him in its pursuit.

We return to the story of Abraham's dream when he was ninety-nine and Sarah was ninety. God once again appeared to Abraham and promised him a son by his wife, Sarah. Abraham had a hard time believing it because of his and Sarah's ages. God assured him that by the following year his promised son, Isaac, would be born. True to the promise, Sarah became pregnant and gave birth to Isaac.

The story didn't stop there, however. Years later when

Isaac was a young boy, God once again appeared to Abraham, and His request was horrifying. He told Abraham to take Isaac to the top of a mountain and kill him on an altar of sacrifice. Abraham dutifully obeyed, and when Isaac was placed on the altar bound and ready to be sacrificed by his father, God intervened and told Abraham to set Isaac free. A ram caught in a thicket was offered on the altar of sacrifice, and Isaac was released to grow into the son of promise. Abraham's dream came true.

Two more lessons can be gleaned from Abraham's story. The first is that God really will help us fulfill any dream He has encouraged us to believe. He will do so in spite of the odds and in spite of the limitations we see around us or in us. Abraham and Sarah gave birth to a miracle baby. For some of us, the dream will take a miracle from God. Abraham's story encourages us to trust that God will provide one, if necessary. However, we should not wait in the wings for God to super-naturally produce a miracle. We must believe that trusting and obeying what God instructs us to do through His Word will produce miraculous results. Our efforts must be focused on living lives that are obedient to His direction, one day at a time, as Abraham did.

Possibly the most difficult aspect of a dream is that when it comes true, we grasp it too tightly. This part of the story may make us wince. How could God have required Abraham to kill his son? Was He teasing him or what? No, God was not teasing—He was testing. The ordered sacrifice of Isaac was God's way of testing Abraham's heart. Was Abraham's dream of a son so important that its fulfillment became more impor-tant than Abraham's obedience to God? Dreams are powerful motivators, so powerful that if we are not careful, their pursuit or fulfillment can become our god. Abraham, unlike many of us, passed the test.

"I guess I wanted a close family more than I thought," Sharon declared. "It has been my main goal for life. I never dreamed that it could interfere with my relationship with God or that it could become more important than God."

Sharon Carpenter's dream of a close family was a good one. But she needed to make sure her willingness to follow God was more important than the dream she so desperately pursued. Re-creating family requires that we embrace a healthy dream of fulfillment. But even then the dream, no matter how fine or good, can never compete with our desire for God. If it does, the dream will not fulfill our deepest needs. Love hunger can make the need for love an idol in our lives.

The good news is that God realizes this and offers His remedy for our need. If we embrace Him first and foremost, love hunger and misplaced desires will not rule us and produce failure. Instead, we will be filled to overflowing with His love and the healthy love of others. As we continue to pursue the insights and methods of healthy family love, let us not forget that His love and desires must be first. He will offer each of us a healthy family dream to pursue and furthermore will assist in its attainment if we, like Abraham, but trust and obey.

A word of caution: we must make sure our dreams, no matter how seemingly appropriate, are never forced on others. Each person must develop and pursue a dream. We can encourage and support others, but we cannot give them a dream. People must forge their own dreams of life, love, and family, or they will end up like Ted Whitman, living a life fraught with frustration and unfulfillment.

A New Dream

"What is a healthy family dream? What does one look like?" Philip Carpenter asked.

Obviously, each person's dream will have its own uniqueness. Some dream of growing up, studying, and choosing a vocation that will support them and their families. Others hope to marry faithfully, have children, educate them, and launch them into life. Still others may dream of remaining single, avoiding the power of lust, and joyfully fellowshipping with others. There are as many facets to a dream as there are individuals who dream. In Abraham's story there were lessons for us in how to develop and manage a dream but little direction on what a dream should be. I believe dreams have this unique flavor to them. What is prized by one may be valued slightly by another. Each of us has a destiny and desires. Abraham's dream was a son. Your dream may be of a daughter.

However, when it comes to family dreams, there seems to be one common theme—wanting a close family. Closeness in a family is usually indicative of shared love and concern. Most of us want a family and marriage wherein love flows freely and peace abounds, a family where conflict is kept to a minimum and loyalty and fidelity are prized. We want to feel secure in the knowledge that we are appreciated and valued. We want to know it and feel it. Closeness is the quality that seems to denote this characteristic in families.

Sharon Carpenter wants a close family because that means experiencing the sharing and intimacy she craves. Closeness in a family provides strength, assurance, and security. To be close requires that we be able to emotionally connect with another in a way that assures shared love, affection, and value. In a world fraught with uncertainties and relational failures, being close wards off anxieties and creates a sense of oneness with others. I believe that is why most family dreams have this key component that addresses how close or far from others the person desires to be. More than any other characteristic of family life, the need for closeness will determine the patterns of giving and getting love that make up the family dream.

The Re-Created Family

As we have learned, dreams of what we hope for in a family are part of the infrastructure of family life. They motivate us to action. Re-creating family requires us to examine the family dream we have adopted. This dream of family is the foundation for how we develop family patterns of love and closeness. If the dream has been marred by the losses and wounds of the past, we need to fashion a new one, making sure we do so in partnership with God.

The re-created family has adopted a new dream for the future that is not distorted by the past. The new dream will embrace healthy patterns of closeness that fulfill the need for love and re-create a legacy of healthy bonding and love fulfillment for future generations. However, the past must be resolved before this new and healthier dream can be embraced.

In the next chapter you will learn how to assure that the obstacles from your past do not interfere with the new dreams and patterns of love that you are fashioning with God.

CHAPTER 12

Stepping Back in Order to Go Forward

*I will seek what was lost and bring back
what was driven away, bind up the broken
and strengthen what was sick.*

—Ezekiel 34:16

The existing family dream holds a key to re-creating a new and healthy future for us and our loved ones. Family dreams are shaped by many influences, especially by the losses and wounds we experience. That means within each dream are seeds of both fulfillment and destruction. If we can un-cover and eliminate the destructive influences, we can easily reshape the dream. To do so requires identification and resolve of the hurtful losses and wounds of the past. Both sources create a love hunger in us that can distort the family dream and produce unhealthy patterns of giving and getting love. We must consciously step back in the past and resolve the losses and wounds that keep us from grabbing hold of the future.

Sharon Carpenter's relationship with her father was her major stumbling block. She craved the love, care, attention, and affirmation a dad provides for a daughter. A daughter needs a dad to love her. A dad not only loves and protects but also disciplines and guides. When a little girl doesn't feel the warmth and caring strength of her dad, a deep loss is registered within. The resultant father wound made Sharon's need for the perfect family too powerful. Her lack of fathering created a love hunger that produced unhealthy love patterns and pressure.

Philip's lack of healthy love, affection, and affirmation from his dad made his family dream and love patterns unhealthy. His approach to his relationship with Sharon was imbalanced, lacking the intimacy and commitment to communication that a healthy marriage requires. His discipline of the children was deficient. Philip's wounded past kept him from giving and getting the love he and his new family needed.

For Ted Whitman, the forces that impelled him to unhealthy fulfillment of another's dream were the unsettled losses of his past. Though his brother had died over twenty years before and his father over ten years, Ted had not finished grieving the losses. Deep in his heart he still pined over losing them and the death of their dream. He was afraid to bond closely with Dodie or the kids for fear of the pain he would feel should he lose them. Connecting with a stranger on a superficial level was much safer than opening his heart to those who loved him most. The consequence was a disengaged style of relating that affected his marriage, his children, and his financial situation.

When we don't let go of the past, we are unable to catch hold of the future. The Carpenters and the Whitmans were partially stuck in the past, unable to fully embrace new dreams and directions. They needed to identify and resolve the losses and wounds of the past that interfered with the pursuit of their dreams and desired patterns of love.

Making Your Loss a Gain

Loss is an inevitable part of life. At one time or another all of us will experience loss. These losses can hinder our growth and destiny, or they can be stepping-stones to fulfillment—it all depends on how we respond to them. Fully resolving a loss releases the sway of the past over the present. Not doing so hinders our ability to embrace God's dream for us.

Ted never fully grieved the loss of his brother, his dad, or the dream they shared. His family had always encouraged keeping a stiff upper lip, conveying the message that "grown men don't cry." As a result, Ted never allowed himself to cry. Twenty years later, the tears were still there and needed to get out. He was still stuck in the past trying to fulfill his dad's dream. Loss is like that. It doesn't go away until we work through it.

Since the work of Dr. Elisabeth Kübler-Ross with people who were dying brought world attention to the grief process, many researchers have studied it. Though her research focused on the bereavement of people who were dying and their families, its conclusions can be applied to any loss.

A loss can involve a person, place, or thing. A loss can be the lack of required love, attention, affection, affirmation, and acceptance. Often the intangible losses of love or concern cause us the most difficulty. Though deeply affected by their lack or loss, we tend to deny their power, try to forget about it, and go on. The result is like scar tissue, which is not as resilient or pliable as healthy tissue. It is hard and brittle. It produces a decision not to risk again, not to love or care. On the other hand, losses and wounds may produce open sores that cause us to try too hard, give too much, or go too far in trying to soothe the inflamed love hunger.

Perhaps the most important thing Dr. Kübler-Ross found is that healthy grieving needs to accompany any loss for resolution to result. Loss is common to all, but few of us give full expression to the accompanying grief that is necessary for it to be laid to rest. Grief is the means by which people work through feelings about loss. Researchers have found that grief has stages and patterns to its expression. If people do not fully face loss and work through the appropriate stages of grief, they will remain emotionally stuck in the past.

As this truth was discussed in our family group, Ted quickly challenged it. "Does this mean I have to go around blubbering every time I think of them?" Ted queried. "Why can't I just forget about it?"

Embarrassed over his tears, Ted did not want to cry. Remember, his family had always held with keeping a stoic attitude toward life's difficulties. Ted needed encouragement and permission to release his repressed feelings. My advice to him was to cry fully and completely every time he thought of his brother and his father. I also gave him an assignment. I told him to pick out a movie, such as *Ordinary People,* that deals with the loss of a brother and let all the sadness out.

For most, the loss of a loved one or the lack of love from another requires numerous tears before resolve comes. The first days and even months after recognizing the loss can be tearful. Gradually, the tears will come less and less frequently, but they may also come unexpectedly at odd moments, perhaps at seeing a friend or after hitting a bump in the road. All this is natural and healthy. When we lose someone or something precious, we are wounded in our deepest inner parts. If we do not fully express the pain of the wound, our suppressed feelings will motivate us in unhealthy ways and may also cause inappropriate behaviors.

"I must have cried for a week straight," Ted later told me. "It got so bad that Dodie thought I was having a breakdown. It was the movie that did it. I watched it six or seven times. Each time I would sit in the chair and cry again."

"How do you feel now?" I asked.

"The ache is gone. Whatever it was that I would feel every time I got close to Dodie or the kids is gone. Something left me. I don't know how else to explain it."

Ted's intense grieving lessened the inner fear of attachment that was tied to his past. His avoidance of intimate connection to Dodie and the kids was a direct result of his unresolved grief. When he discovered that grief was something he could go through and survive, he no longer feared closely attaching to the ones he loved. His grieving released the roadblock to embracing the healthy family dream and patterns of love he was fashioning.

Grieving the Loss

To remove the roadblocks to the future, each of us must identify the hurtful losses of the past and grieve them. The loss may be of a family member, as it was for Ted. It may be the loss of a father, mother, or family through divorce. It may be more abstract, such as the loss of innocence through being sexually violated. Or it may be the loss of one's childhood due to undeserved responsibilities, pressures, or pain. Whatever the love deficiency of your past, the result was a loss to you.

I never received the verbal blessing of approval from my dad. Expressions such as "I love you," "You are special," or "I'm really proud of you" were never forthcoming. Even though I believed my dad loved me, I never heard the words. The resultant love hunger empowered a family ideal in which I was always telling my kids I loved them. I gave them an excess of what I lacked. My dad's love was distant and unspoken, but mine became excessive and stifling. It was a loss I needed to resolve to re-create healthy patterns of love between my children and me.

Counseling helped the Whitmans and the Carpenters identify their losses and the resulting love patterns. You may also need help from someone. However, many individuals readily see their loss or lack from childhood once they focus on the past and prayerfully ask God to reveal what needs to be healed.

Re-creating family requires identifying the loss. Once you recognize the loss, the following steps will help in successfully completing the grief cycle.

Give Full Vent to Your Tears

Tears are the cleansing agent of the soul. They are the natural response to hurt. We are crying for our loss and feeling our pain. We must give ourselves the permission to cry whenever the tears come. When enough tears have been shed, they will stop coming.

Ted needed encouragement to cry. He also found it comforting and healing to shed his tears before God when the pain came. As the Scripture declares, He will "comfort all who mourn, . . . give them beauty for ashes, the oil of joy for mourning" (Isa. 61:2–3). Many who desire God's comfort do not receive it because they do not cry out to Him in their grief.

Resolve Whatever Anger, Resentment, or Fear Resulted from Your Loss

Anger is a natural part of the reaction to loss. We ask, "Why me?" We are offended by having it happen to us. Losing something we value creates hurt and anger. We may even blame the person for dying or others who contributed to the loss. We may even blame God.

Sharon struggled with anger. "For years I bitterly blamed Kelly's dad and God for the divorce," she explained. "It took our Family Week for me to finally realize I was stuck in blaming others and feeling miserable as a result. Once I realized this, I let go of the anger and cried for three days straight. I think I can now say that I truly forgive him for what he did."

Resolving grief requires us to let go of our anger and indignation at God and others. We must recognize that we are angry and then proceed to vent it and resolve it. Our tears are frequently covered over by anger. If we forgive the offense, the tears will come, and we will begin the deeper healing we need.

Fear can also be a natural reaction to loss. When we lose someone or something we prize, the pain can make us fearful of ever again losing something we value. Sharon's fear of another divorce prompted her to pressure and pursue Philip excessively about his need for change. She was afraid to share her heart with God, fearing He would not grant her the desires of her heart for a fulfilling marriage and close family. Fear is often the underlying motive for self-proclaimed dreams and mistrust of God. When we face the fear and resolve it, our trust in God is reestablished. Fear, not God, is our enemy.

Resist Bargaining and Self-Blame

All too often when we lose something or someone we value, we want to bargain with God and others. But bargaining doesn't work. It is only a postponement tactic to avoid facing the pain and the inevitability of the loss. Sharon's trust problem with God was further compounded by her past efforts at bargaining. As a child she remembered promising God that if He would give her a daddy, she would do anything God wanted her to do. The daddy never materialized, and her disappointment in God grew.

Self-blame is also common. We blame ourselves for not preventing the loss, not being better, nicer, or more able to have foreseen it. Ted frequently questioned himself, wondering what he could have done to keep the dream alive and make it work.

Self-blame is another stage we must face and work through. If we blame ourselves for a loss, we will avoid accepting it and learning from it. This avoidance tactic will encourage us to remain in self-pity. Self-pity encourages a victim mentality, thus limiting our options for growth and change. Even if we are responsible for the loss, we must accept the fallibility, learn from it, and move on.

Fully Accept Your Loss

No one desires loss. It hurts to lack something, and it can be devastating to lose someone. Full acceptance does not mean that we would have freely chosen the loss; rather, since it has occurred, we should accept it and become the better for it. The losses we feel most deeply in life show where our security has been invested. We all tend to place our security in people, places, and things instead of God.

Until he resolved his loss, Ted was unable to see past his family dream and trust that God would provide him with another one. "I'm more accepting of what happened," Ted said. "I feel I am also getting along better with Dodie, the kids, and even God."

"Do you have a new dream?" I asked.

"Yeah. I think so. It's not fully formed, but I think the first part of it is that I can be happy with the family God has given me instead of chasing happiness everywhere else. I was never content with just staying at home or doing things with the family. I'm also getting my head screwed on better about work. I think I need to take those vocational tests you recommended in order to see what jobs I might handle better."

Ted's acceptance not only strengthened his relationships with family and God but also offered new hope. Accepting losses is a potent step toward the future. It is also a reinvestment of our security in God. It is a profound acknowledgment of His right to be God and our need to trust in Him even when we don't understand our circumstances. Total acceptance is full acknowledgment of the loss coupled with an ability to say, "It is well with my soul." Acceptance releases us to new possibilities as it did with Ted. Total acceptance of a loss takes time, tears, and God's help.

As in Ted's case, many losses are connected with valued intangibles. The losses of love, camaraderie, affection, attention, and care are the intangible losses that deeply affect us, as are the losses of self-esteem, position, power, and status. The problem with these abstract losses is that we deny their presence and never fully work through their result. Ted never realized how the losses of his brother, dad, and family dream affected him. He needed to cry over losing his dad and brother and also over losing the dream. Once recognized, faced, and mourned, an intangible loss will lose its power, freeing the person to embrace healthier ways of loving and living.

Healing Other Wounds

There are other wounds besides losses that we need to face and resolve. Any type of emotional wound can empower an unhealthy dream. Losses are among the most common types of wounds we experience, but many events in life that we normally don't associate with losses can wound the inner being. For example, betrayal, rejection, abuse, and harsh criticism can wound us. Favoritism, neglect, and inappropriate discipline are but a sampling of things that can hurt the inner being. Inner wounds are not always visible, but they are there and they affect our lives. Unless they are healed, they will result in unhealthy dreams and love patterns. Resolving these wounds requires revisiting them and releasing the pain. For healing to take place, the painful feelings associated with the memories or event need to be released. The painful feelings empower the negative patterns.

Bill Haskell came from a small town. He, like Philip Carpenter and so many other men of his generation, was raised by an authoritarian father. His dad was a rugged outdoorsman and rancher who severely punished Bill as a child. In one of our counseling sessions I asked Bill if he felt any hurt or resentment as a result of his father's harsh discipline and lack of affection. Bill denied feeling anything but admiration for his dad.

His wife, Peggy, however, had different feelings: "It makes me mad every time I think about how mean his dad was to him. I still have a hard time believing Bill when he says it doesn't bother him. I have wondered if that is why Bill has been so hard on Bill, Junior. The two of them don't get along."

It took Bill months of counseling before he could acknowledge how hurt he was as a result of his father's harsh discipline and lack of affectionate concern. When I first explained it to him, his response was a superficial "I didn't know he did anything wrong to me. But if you say so, I'll forgive him right now." I challenged him to dig deeper—to truly wrestle with the issue until he felt the feelings. Bill tended to minimize the hurt of his past, thinking that if he didn't make a big deal of it, it wouldn't affect him. Denying or minimizing what hurt him only assures that it will continue to affect him.

Don't Minimize

Healing wounds requires that people not minimize what has happened. Most people have a tendency to make light of past events that have hurt them. Even though they may not have fully realized the impact of the event at the time it happened, careful evaluation in the present can determine its effect on their lives. Complete and fearless reexamination of the wound is the only path to full healing.

When facing wounds, you must distinguish your wrongdoing and wrong responses from others' wrongdoing and offenses against you. Do not make excuses for people who have rejected or wounded you in some way, but do your best to forgive them for the harm they have caused and cost you. Parents, brothers, sisters, and others are imperfect. All families wound each other. Some do it knowingly and even maliciously, but most do not. Regardless of the reason, the wound is real and needs to be acknowledged without excuse. More times than I can count I hear clients say, "My folks did the best they could," thereby closing the door to further exploration of wounds and their repercussions.

Too often we are tempted to excuse or justify the sins or offenses others commit against us. True healing and true forgiveness require full recognition of the violation before resolution is possible. There can be no true forgiveness when we minimize or deny the offense. When we deny the hurt, we suppress the wound and can't really forgive. Bill has not fully forgiven his father because he has minimized the offense.

Offer True Forgiveness

Forgiveness is really a letting go of the past. It is a decision to allow God to be God and not insist that things be our way. Forgiveness is a deep and profound recognition of others' wrongdoing against us. In forgiveness, we have to face our humanness—and that of others—and decide not to let sin or wrongdoing win. True forgiveness lets go of the pain, releases the wrongdoing, accepts the outcome, and goes on with life better for the experience. This is why true forgiveness is so rare. Most of us don't fully forgive, and we become the less for it: less loving, less giving, and less caring.

I had not seen Bill Haskell for a few weeks due to a business trip he had taken. When we met for counseling, Bill surprised me.

"I think I now know what you've been saying to me," he explained. "I've been in Albuquerque for the past two weeks on business and have had plenty of time to think about what you've said. I remembered the time when I found Mom crying quietly in her room after Dad beat me with a stick. It was then I decided never to let his harshness bother me so that it wouldn't bother Mom. I broke down and cried. I guess I cried for her and also for me. Dad was too hard and uncaring.

And it did hurt me and my mom. I've always known it but have never been able to admit it to myself or anyone else. After a couple of days I visited a small prayer chapel and told God all about it. I asked Him to help me forgive and start over. I don't want to repeat the pattern of pain my dad caused us."

Real forgiveness does not pretend. It is for real wounds. True forgiveness starts with choosing to forgive despite the pain. That was the choice Bill made while in Albuquerque. It was his decision to release the hurt of the past to guarantee the success of the future.

But what if the others haven't changed? Are we still to forgive? Forgiveness does not wait for others to change. There is no demand or expectation in forgiveness, only release. It is giving up the claim to justice. It is releasing others from the debt of wrongdoing they owe us. At its best, it is unconditional.

Finally, forgiveness is a promise to ourselves and others not to bring up the offense to them ever again, not to tell others about it, and not to nurse or rehearse it in our thoughts. This kind of forgiveness is healing to us and to others. It is a rare gift we offer to ourselves and others, and it is free for them, even though there's a price of humility, self-examination, and effort required of us. When others have really wronged us, real forgiveness takes time. The times when we receive grace and are released in an instant are wonderful, and we can be thankful for them; but God doesn't seem to have set life up to be a breeze all the time. There would be no character building in that kind of arrangement. The gift of forgiveness is that it releases us from the tyranny of the past and the potential failure of the future.

Take Full Responsibility

Every action of another calls forth a response in us. Our only assurance of health and healing is to reexamine our responses to the wounds caused by others and take full responsibility for our actions and reactions.

Rarely do individuals respond positively to a wounding situation. The pain and power of a wound usually provoke the worst in us rather than the best. We make faulty judgments about what happened and vow to ourselves that we will never be hurt again. Without realizing it, we allow the wound to change us in negative ways, becoming angry, bitter, and resentful or even fearful, self-pitying, and ashamed. We may become overly hungry and demanding of love. Or we may become withdrawn and depressed or vindictive and abusive. To keep these wrong reactions from controlling us, we must not only forgive the offense but retract the empowering inner vows we make to ourselves as a result.

A vow is a pledge to oneself to act in a certain manner. Ted Whitman vowed to "never let his father down." After his brother died, Ted redoubled his efforts to encourage his dad to go ahead with the project—all to no avail. His vow set in motion a pattern of taking too much responsibility for the dreams of others and not enough responsibility for discovering his own destiny. Ted needed to recant his vow, understanding that God had not called him to a life of service to other men's dreams. Once he asked God to forgive him, the burden for helping others too much decreased, and he became more relationally and financially responsible to his family.

Unhealthy patterns are usually responses to a wound that hasn't been resolved. For example, when Bill Haskell was a teenager, his first girlfriend betrayed him by sleeping with another guy the summer he was working his uncle's ranch in Montana. Bill vowed never to allow a woman to hurt him that way again. He also vowed to get whatever sex he could from the women he dated. His response to her rejection caused him to use women sexually, to give them love only when it meant he would get sex in return. Healing the pattern required that he recant the vows he had made and repent of his wrongdoing by asking for God's forgiveness. Doing so broke the power of the pattern and freed him once again to develop healthy ways of relating to women. Health and healing cannot come without the willingness to take full responsibility before God and others for actions and reactions.

Invite the Memories

The last step in healing wounds is to invite to remembrance any memories that are still painful. When hurtful memories surface and are faced anew, healing comes. Don't be afraid of old memories. If you are in a safe place, you can handle now what you couldn't then. If what you experienced is too scary or painful to handle alone, find a close friend, member of the clergy, or qualified therapist to help. As you relive the memory, invite God to be there with you. You need others, and you need Him. He will provide you with the true perspective of what happened and what needs to be done. He also will empower the change.

Tell Him how you honestly feel. I have shared my deepest feelings and wounds with God many times, and I have yet to be disappointed in the outcome. He specializes in healing broken hearts and setting captives free. As you share your innermost feelings and thoughts, He will comfort you; and as you do so, take full responsibility for your actions, judgments, and vows. Confessing them to Him releases you.

Also share with Him the names of those who have hurt you, how they hurt you, and what you did in response. Ask Him to take the pain away. Affirm your forgiveness of them, and ask God to forgive them for the pain they have caused you. Doing so will cleanse the wound and allow proper healing to occur. Finally, thank Him for His help and forgiveness.

Grieving your losses and healing your wounds release you from the tyranny of the past. You have the opportunity to create new and healthier dreams and patterns of loving. You are empowered to re-create family in ways that assure that you will give and get the love you need.

In the following chapter we will explore how to develop a game plan for assuring that your efforts will succeed in creating a healthy future for your children and your children's children.

CHAPTER 13

The
Re-Created
Family

Most people do not really listen with the
intent to understand; rather, they listen with
the intent to reply.

—Stephen Covey

Unhealthy relationship patterns are the culprit in the struggle for getting and giving love. These ingrained ways of relating rob us of vital relationship. They can negatively influence the choice of a spouse, the management of marriage, and the parenting of children. Like mighty fortresses that withstand change, these relational strongholds can even cause family members to repeat mistakes or behaviors that they know are hurtful.

Our goal must be to create healthy family patterns of love by overcoming the unhealthy ones. Re-creating family is reconstructing these relational patterns so that family members give and get the healthy love they need. The most difficult first step is spotting the pattern. Then we can break its power and implement new and healthier ways of giving and getting love, ways that will ensure stable marriages, loving families, and healthy children.

Characteristics of Re-Created Families

Emily Sooter is the eighty-four-year-old grandmother of one of our Family Week clients. Shortly after a lecture, Emily started our next session by asking, "How do you know when you're finished re-creating your family?" The question strikes at the heart of what healthy family life is all about. Re-creating family is a journey, not a destination. I believe we are never finished shaping and reshaping our families and their legacies. The challenge of family life is always to create a new and healthier future out of the legacy of the past.

A re-created family has come to accept the need to continually evaluate its patterns of love in a manner that does not encourage blame or morbid introspection. It is best characterized by the willingness of family members to recognize their deficiencies and commit to change. Even in the healthiest families there will always be struggle and the need to adapt and change. Families in reconstruction are imperfect families made of imperfect members who have the courage to pursue a dream for something better. The re-created family is on an endless journey that becomes more and more fruitful.

This has been Susan's and my experience, as it has been for many families we have worked with. What has changed in us has been not only our patterns of love but our attitudes toward family and each other. We now have a generational perspective of life. We want to love better for the present benefits and also for the help it will be to our future generations. We have come to recognize our individual legacies of deficient love, and we are consciously working toward offering an improved legacy of love to our children. The change of attitude does not mean that we don't struggle over closeness in our marriage or repeat the unhealthy styles of discipline that come so naturally to us. We are still imperfect, even though we have changed. However, we have come to see our struggles and conflicts as potentially helpful instead of hindering.

Healthy Conflict

Conflicts play a major role in promoting or hindering the ability to re-create family life. A redemptive attitude toward conflict is a benchmark of re-created families. Re-created families still have conflict, but their attitude and response to conflict have changed.

Emily Sooter again blessed us with her wisdom by describing how she and her deceased husband, Jake, viewed conflict: "Jake and I never minded a good argument. We knew that whenever we clashed, there was something to be learned by both of us. We didn't expect things to work without a good fight."

Working and living with other people have a way of bringing out the best—and the worst—in us. Conflict can be healthy in a relationship. The love, care, and concern we need should be balanced with challenge, sacrifice, and difficulty. "As iron sharpens iron," the Scripture says, "so a man sharpens the countenance of his friend" (Prov. 27:17). An ax head produces sparks when sharpened against a grinding wheel. A healthy marital or familial conflict can also sharpen rough edges despite the sparks that fly. In healthy relationships we not only love and care but also strengthen and challenge. Conflict, managed rightly, makes us stretch beyond our self-centeredness, requiring us to push past our comfort levels and learn how to sacrificially love another. It can grow us up if we allow it to.

As I have shared, Susan and I have had plenty of conflict in our marriage. We have gone back and forth over how close to be as well as how to discipline the children. I tend toward enmeshed and codependent ways of giving and getting love. Susan is more apt to remain disengaged and counter-dependent. I've been the permissive parent, and she has been the authoritarian one. When we realized that our conflicts could teach each of us more about ourselves and make us healthier, our patterns changed. Instead of pressuring and per-suading Susan about how I was right and she was wrong, I adopted an attitude that assumed we were probably both right and wrong. This attitude freed me to listen to her and learn from our confrontations. Susan also changed, becoming more willing to accept my input and defend less. The shifts in atti-tude and behavior were prompted by our hard-won insights, and they made all the difference.

The re-created family understands the shaping influences of its members, thus accepting more and blaming less. I have come to appreciate aspects of Susan's tendency toward disen-gagement. She thinks independently and can always be counted on for an objective opinion. There are also strength in her independence and value in the ways in which she has challenged our children to grow up and take care of them-selves. I would have protected them too much for too long. However, there is also a need for someone like me in her life who is better at initiating and maintaining the intimacy marriage needs. I've also helped her define and work with the kids' feeling issues. We are good for each other.

Conflict and differences can be blessings in disguise. Characteristic behaviors in others produce predictable responses in us. Each conflict or crisis we face brings to the surface what is resident deep within. Round-robin disputes and repetitious patterns should be signposts. Like two sore thumbs touching, each person's reaction is being fueled by the inner stronghold of fear, insecurity, hurt, or anger. This has been true in Susan's and my relationship and in the marriages and families we have counseled.

Ownership

The good news is that as we accept more ownership for our behavior, the patterns and strongholds can give way to healing and change *if we are willing*. This is one of the most crucial and difficult aspects about conquering our deficient patterns and making sure we don't pass them on to our children. When we use the conflicts of life and relationship to show us *what needs to change in us,* healing comes. Obviously, that doesn't mean the other person doesn't need to change, too, but as I've said, our task should be to focus first on how we can change, not how someone else needs to.

This wisdom is also helpful in dealing with children for whom we are responsible. If we can first deal with ourselves, we will be better able to deal with them in healthy ways that promote needed changes in them. Our eldest daughter was repeating my patterns of codependent love with her friends at school. My overprotectiveness and Susan's disengagement were encouraging her codependence. When Susan and I changed, she became less codependent.

Truth in Love

Too often we don't deal with family members or ourselves in a truthful manner. Studies of family life indicate that being truthful in a loving and appropriate way is a common characteristic of healthy families. But hurtful communication and denial of truth are major traits of unhealthy families. Truth without love is destructive. So is love without truth.

Members of a re-created family commit to sharing truth with each other in a loving way. When honest, open, and caring communication is present in a family, healthy expressions of love emerge. Our special Family Week programs teach family members how to do this with each other. When they communicate, they are able to resolve the problems and patterns that hinder members from getting and giving love.

Tools for Re-Creating Family

The remainder of this chapter offers you tools to re-create the patterns in your family. These exercises provide guided steps to be both more truthful and more loving. The seven exercises will assist you in translating what you have read about into action. I have used these exercises in working with countless couples and families. They have been very effective in changing unhealthy patterns.

Some of the exercises require considerable courage and honesty, which is one reason they work so well. Maybe only one or a few members of your family want to do the exercises. That is not unusual. As a rule of thumb, disengaged individuals have less motivation to work on relational problems, and enmeshed individuals have a greater desire. Motivated family members can still benefit from working through the exercises.

As you will see, one key tool is the preparation of a "Truth in Love List." This list is an inventory that will assist you in evaluating the communication needs of your family and help you share them in a truthful and loving manner. Working through this list will be helpful for an individual to do, regardless of whether or not there's an opportunity to share the list with a spouse or family members. Completing the list can bring insight, especially if it's used in conjunction with the "Prayer List."

Certain exercises require a substantial time commitment and a commitment to change. It is therefore important that each person consciously evaluate motives and make a commitment to change through personal growth. Children and teenagers may resist doing this. Some families have made Exercise 7 optional, while others have considered it mandatory. Unless there are serious resistance and rebellion in your child, mandatory participation can be helpful. If you have doubts about requiring a family member to participate, get advice from a wise counselor or clergy person. Be aware that there is always resistance to change. If people are willing to risk change, however, the obvious benefits will usually encourage their continued participation.

The Right Motivation

Because the process of change can be uncomfortable and even wounding, you need to clearly examine your motivations. Is your motive for doing the exercises wanting to prove that another person is wrong and you are right? If so, doing the exercises will be hurtful instead of helpful. When you share your thoughts and feelings with another person, do so with the goal of helping both parties *win*. When we share innermost thoughts or feelings, we become vulnerable. It is important to handle that vulnerability by not using it as ammunition against another.

It is best to start with the first exercise and proceed in sequence to the last since each exercise builds on the previous one. In the Appendix is a feelings list, which is provided for individuals who may have difficulty identifying how they truly feel.

Healthy families value each member's feelings and thoughts. Unhealthy families may never affirm or allow an opportunity for healthy expression of feelings. Susan and I have witnessed countless miracles of change when feelings are openly shared and resolved. Re-created families work through each member's feelings using healthy communication. Many exercises require you to assess and identify your feelings, so use the feelings list as an aid. You may want to write your answers in a notebook, but remember to keep your notes in a safe place. As you explore these issues, keep what you do confidential so that your fear of exposure will not hinder your honesty.

Professional Help

Family problems and issues can be very difficult for a family to overcome. The exercises and steps shared here may be too much for an individual or a family to handle. Counseling may be necessary before family members are willing or able to open their hearts and risk the vulnerability re-creating family requires. If you need professional help, don't hesitate to seek it. Many qualified Christian counselors know how God heals individuals and families. Our counseling center retains a partial listing of therapists from different parts of the country. If you desire information on our special Family Week programs or need a referral, contact us at House of Hope Counseling Services, 8010 East McDowell, Suite B-212, Scottsdale, Arizona 85257.

Exercise 1: An Examination of Closeness

Purpose:

To analyze your past and present patterns of closeness.

Suggestions:

If you have any questions about how disengaged or enmeshed you may have been or are, ask for input. Other family members can help you assess yourself. Also refer to the chapters of the book that describe these two polarities of closeness. Reviewing the material can help you better evaluate yourself.

Instructions:

1. Review and evaluate your family of origin (Mom, Dad, siblings, close relatives, adoptive parents, etc.). Make a list of each family member, caretaker, and meaningful friend you had while growing up. On a scale of one to ten, with ten being too close and one being too distant, evaluate each relationship, determining whether you were more disengaged or enmeshed with each person.

2. Review and evaluate your current family members (spouse, in-laws, children, etc.) as well as family-of-origin members still alive. Determine on a scale of one to ten how close or distant you now are with each one.

3. Answer the following questions:

• Which persons were you closest to? Farthest from?

• Which persons did you want to be close to? Why?

- Were you more enmeshed or disengaged?

- Have any of the relationships changed? If so, how and why?

- What are your feelings regarding your past bonding patterns?

- What has this exercise shown you about yourself?

Exercise 2: Generational Review

Purpose:

To further recognize the generational influences that have contributed to your patterns of loving and caring.

Suggestions:

This book has revealed numerous ways parents and families can affect the future relationship patterns of their children. Parental bonding patterns, styles of discipline, marriage roles, parental wounds, and surrogate partnerships are but a few of the many influences. Courageously evaluate your family tree. Remember the intent of this exercise is not to blame but to heal.

Instructions:

1. How has being too close to or too distant from your mom, dad, and other caretakers affected your need for closeness? Has this caused relational problems for you? If so, how?

2. How did your mom's and dad's management of their marriage(s) affect your need for closeness? Were you a surrogate partner or parent, or were you ignored? Describe what happened. Also evaluate whether or not you have parented or partnered your children.

3. How did your mom's, dad's, or caretakers' style of dis-

cipline affect you? What styles of discipline do you see in other members of your family tree? Have you repeated any of these hurtful styles with your children? What other parenting errors or wounds have you experienced? What have you passed on to your children?

4. What generational patterns of closeness or distance do you see in your family tree (parents, grandparents, great-grandparents, uncles, aunts, siblings)?

5. What factors from the past (divorce, loss, etc.) may have empowered or started the unhealthy patterns? Guess if you are not sure.

6. What personal strongholds of fear, anger, self-pity, shame, addiction, sexual lust, and so on are in your family tree?

7. Which family strongholds and patterns are present in your life? Your children's lives? Your grandchildren's lives?

Exercise 3: Prayer List

Purpose:

To empower the work of change through prayer.

Suggestions:

John Wesley once commented, "God does everything through prayer and nothing without it." Prayer is our primary weapon in tearing down spiritual strongholds that have empowered the hurtful patterns. Accountability and responsibility begin first with God, through prayer, before they extend to others. Without God's assistance, each of us is alone in trying to change the powerful, ingrained patterns that have endured the generations. As we humble ourselves before Him in prayer, He will grace us with the power needed for change.

Instructions:

1. Review your family tree, making a list of family members who have demonstrated patterns of disengagement and enmeshment. Also list individuals who were involved in unhealthy surrogate partnerships.

2. List the generational styles of discipline that have been unhealthy and wounding, also listing the individuals' names beside their patterns.

3. List the factors (divorce, loss, anger, fear, etc.) you discovered in your family tree analysis that may have empowered the generational strongholds.

4. Make a separate list of patterns and strongholds of relating and parenting that you have passed on to your children and grandchildren.

5. Set aside a minimum of seven minutes a day for seven days to pray about each of the above. Read Nehemiah 1:6–11, and use the same pattern of prayer when you pray. Prayerfully repent of the sins and mistakes of your family line and of those you have committed. Forgive people who have hurt you, and ask God to break the power of the strongholds and change the patterns.

Exercise 4: Amends List

Purpose:

To take responsibility for what you have done to others in order to facilitate reconciliation and change.

Suggestions:

Making amends is the way you can take responsibility for your actions with others. Making an amend requires admitting to the other person your wrongdoing (whether intentional or not) in a humble but not a groveling manner. When you make amends, also include what you want from the person in return, usually understanding or forgiveness or both.

Instructions:

1. Following the sample, list every amend you need to make to family members or significant others.

Sample

List amends that you need to make for your past behavior.

- Identify what you did or didn't do that you are making amends for. *(Example:* "I'm so sorry for all the years I was too busy working to give you the love, time, and care that you needed and deserved from me.")

- Be specific. *(Example:* "I remember last year when you wanted to take a few days with me on a mini-vacation and I told you I was too busy at work.")

- Describe how you think it must have made the person feel. *(Example:* "It must have hurt you deeply that I made my work more important than you and our marriage.")

- Ask for forgiveness. *(Example:* "Would you please forgive me for this hurt? I promise to be more sensitive to your needs.")

2. In listing your amends, take full responsibility for what you've done, and try to identify how your wrongdoing must have made the person feel. Use the feeling list (see Appendix) if necessary.

3. Save your list to use in Exercise 7.

Exercise 5: Wounds and Offenses List

Purpose:

To work toward new patterns of love through resolving offenses and wounds from the past.

Suggestions:

Not only do you need to share your shortcomings, but you also need to lovingly confront others over theirs. This "Wounds and Offenses List" offers you the opportunity to face and resolve the things that others have knowingly or unknowingly done to wound you.

Instructions:

1. Following the sample, list all the ways the other person or family member has wounded or offended you. Refer to the feeling list if necessary to ensure that you are able to say exactly how the wound or offense made you *feel.*

Sample

List wounds and/or offenses you have regarding the other person (things the person said, did, or didn't do that you disliked and that hurt you).

- Describe the event that hurt or offended you. *(Example:* "Do you remember the time last Christmas when we had an argument and you left home?")

- State how it made you feel. Start with "I feel" or "I felt." *(Example:* "I felt abandoned, fearful, hurt.")

- Tell the person what you need or expect as a result of this. *(Example:* "I need for you to know how I feel and for us to talk things out from now on rather than you running away and leaving home and my not knowing where you are.'')

2. Prioritize your list by listing the most hurtful or serious wounds or offenses first and the lesser ones last.

3. Save the list for Exercise 7.

Exercise 6: Affirmations List

Purpose:

To share affection, appreciation, and love in a caring and direct manner.

Suggestions:

Some family members never affirm each other by sharing directly how much they appreciate or love another. All families and relationships have positive aspects that members can and should share with each other. This exercise helps families balance out the negative with positive "I care" messages.

Instructions:

1. Following the sample, list the things you like about a person. Make sure your list of positives has no less than ten items on it.

Sample

List affirmations or appreciations you want to share with the other person (things that you appreciate about behavior or qualities and characteristics that you like).

• Describe your appreciation. *(Example:* "I like it when you share your feelings with me.")

• Be specific. *(Example:* "Last summer when we went to the beach, you shared with me for over an hour.")

- State how you felt as a result. *(Example:* "I felt close to you. I felt loved and appreciated by you.")

2. Prioritize your affirmations, saving the best *for last.* Again, use the feeling list if necessary to get the right words.

3. Save your affirmations for Exercise 7.

Exercise 7: Truth in Love Lists

Purpose:

To break down the walls of the past, diffuse current tensions, and create new patterns for getting and giving love.

Suggestions:

Sharing "Truth in Love Lists" is the culmination of the other exercises. Your "Truth in Love" inventory involves the work you did on amends (Exercise 4), wounds and offenses (Exercise 5), and affirmations (Exercise 6). By sharing your lists, you are attempting to take full responsibility for your wrongdoing (amends), face others with theirs (wounds and offenses), yet still share with them how much you care for and appreciate them (affirmations). This combination is a powerful agent for change.

To effectively do this exercise, you must *precisely* follow the guidelines. "Truth in Love Lists" cover tender territory. They have the potential of bringing many feelings to the surface. Before attempting this exercise, choose a safe place where you will not be interrupted. Set aside at least an hour and a half to two hours—more if more than two people are involved. If you know that sharing your lists could create explosive emotions, find a qualified facilitator to help—one who has had training and experience in conflict resolution and active listening.

Instructions:

1. Start the session with prayer, choosing one person to be the *listener* and the other the person to share the list.

2. The person who shares first must *start with amends*. To share means not to hide anything but also not to hurl insults or accusations at the other person. The purpose of this exercise is for both of you to attack the problem, not each other. Sharing entails sharing feelings and facts to truly discover what is deep within your hearts. The person sharing must be vulnerable and use "I" messages instead of "You did _____ to me." The following are examples of "I" messages:

- "I become hurt and angry when you yell at me."

- "I need to make amends for what I've done."

- "I feel good when I'm around you."

"I" messages assure your partner that you are not blaming but are taking responsibility for how you feel and think.

3. While one person shares, the other must *actively listen*. Active listening requires whoever is listening to not be on the *defensive*. The listener must adopt an interview style, asking questions of the person sharing to make sure the other person's true feelings and thoughts are being fully explored. After a thought has been expressed, the listener must *summarize* to the sharer what was said. The one sharing then confirms or corrects the summary. Sharing and summarizing assure that real communication occurs.

The listener may also probe for meaning to find out what the person is feeling—to truly know what is in the person's heart. *At no time should the listener explain anything* until the person sharing has completed that portion of the list.

Once the sharer has completed the amends, the listener is entitled to *briefly respond*. The *sharer* then must *summarize* to the listener what was heard.

4. After the first person has finished sharing the "Amends List," the roles reverse, and the one who shared now becomes the listener and vice versa.

5. Once the sharing and listening of the "Amends Lists" are completed, both people should then go over *wounds and offenses*. Following the same pattern as before, one shares while the other listens and summarizes, then the roles are switched.

6. The *affirmation* work is left for last. Again, one shares while the other listens, and then the roles are reversed.

7. When more than two family members are involved, the list work is completed between two family members at a time while the other members watch but do not interfere. When everyone has finished, the family may choose to close the session in prayer, song, or whatever seems appropriate.

8. When all have shared their lists, there needs to be a time-out from processing what has taken place. This time allows the issues raised by the session to settle and the participants can gain perspective. Further discussion is advisable within a week or so but should *follow the same format of sharing and listening* or else communication will not occur and old negative patterns will emerge.

Note: Susan and I have found it helpful to do mini–"Truth in Love" sessions within our family whenever tensions arise. It is a good way to clear the air and check out how everyone is doing. The children have used it to vent their problems with us as well as with each other. One of our middle children declares that the sessions are boring but appears more light-hearted afterward. After a "Truth in Love" session, relationships improve and the negative patterns diminish.

When families use these tools and adopt the attitudes and practices of re-created families, they experience a release of love. They cease to be consumed by the problems of the past or the demands of the present. The capacity to love is enlarged, and woundedness is diminished. Love is more spontaneous, and crises often become stepping-stones instead of stumbling blocks. The unhealthy patterns of the past no longer rule. Re-created families offer legacies of love that will endure for generations.

My hope is that our journey together has helped you examine and reshape your legacy of love—not only for your benefit but for those you love. We all need love. We seek it in our families, marriages, and friendships. It is the universal quest. The challenge is to create healthy ways of getting and giving love that will endure the test of time. My prayer is that you will experience the true gift of family love that God desires for each of us. Love and blessings as you re-create your family.

LIST OF
FEELINGS

Positive Feelings

Pursuit Feelings (Feelings We Like)

LOVE—a feeling of attraction toward good

Liking of

Affection for

Tenderness toward

Friendly toward

Concern for

Wonder at

Warmth toward

Passion for

Drawn toward

Captivated by

Admiration for

Attracted by

DESIRE

Longing for

Coveting

Impulse toward

Hanker for

Curious

Nosy

Craving for

Need for

Impelled toward

Want

Inquisitive

HOPE

Expectant of

Aspire to

Reliance on

Buoyancy

Confidence

Anticipate

Trust

"Faith" in

Brightness

JOY

Happy

Pleased/pleasant

Satisfied

Refreshed

Completed

Fulfilled

Gratified

Gleeful

Delighted

Calm

Peaceful

Tranquil

Relieved

Comfortable

Contented

COURAGE

Spunk

Bravery

Patience

Toughness

Competence

Bold

Cocky

Guts

Risking

Endurance

Confidence

Assurance

Audacious

Negative Feelings

Avoidance Feelings (Feelings We Don't Like)

HATE—a feeling of revulsion against evil

Dislike of
Cold toward
Indifferent to

Repelled by
Despise
Withdrawn from

AVERSION

Turn away from
Rejection of
Repelled by
Escape
Evade

Craving for
Need for
Impelled toward
Want
Inquisitive

DESPAIR

Hopeless
Desperate
Inevitable
Despondent
Doubtful
Skeptical

Disappointment
Trapped
Concerned
Stopped
Defeated

Helpless
Suspicious
Inadequate
Discouraged
Lost

SORROW

Sad/saddened
Grieved
Depressed
Melancholy
Unhappy
Sorry
Pity
Crushed

Embarrassed
Humiliated
Overwhelmed
Put down
Rejected
Humbled
Disgusted

Dejected
Dour
Wounded
Ashamed
Gloomy
Hurt
Martyred

FEAR

Terror	Panic	Anxiety
Flight	Escape	Nervousness
Alarm	Uneasy	Jumpy
Trepidation	Horror	Appalled
Timid	Cowed	Apprehension
Fright	Cowardly	Worry
Scare	Cautious	Distrust
Mistrust	Startled	Astonished
Restless		

ANGER

Frustrated	Resentment	Irritation
Fury	Mad	Bugged
Rage	Grouchy	Arrogance
Ire	Grumpy	Aggravated
Indignation	Disgruntled	Belligerence

About the Author

Alfred H. Ells is a marriage and family counselor, seminar speaker, and author of several bestselling books, including *One-Way Relationships* and *Released to Love*. He founded House of Hope Counseling Services in Scottsdale, Arizona.